AGAINST DAUNTING ODDS . . .
ONE MAN'S HUNGER FOR THE THRILL OF DISCOVERY . . .
A RICH DEPOSIT OF SILVER GUARDED BY THE HARSH
TERRAIN OF APACHE COUNTRY . . .

**AND SOUTHEASTERN ARIZONA TERRITORY
WOULD NEVER BE THE SAME.**

Lured by Ed Schieffelin's silver strike, enticed by
opportunity — newcomers and old-timers flocked to a
rough mining camp that would become Tombstone.

TOUGH FOLKS, WILD TIMES —
Among the names of Clanton, Earp, and Holliday, there were
others who played their part as the mining camp transformed
into an oasis of frontier decadence and cosmopolitan culture,
reckless violence and luxury. Rubbing shoulders with
legendary heroes and villains, ordinary people lived real life
in extraordinary times. Their true stories are . . .

TOMBSTONE CHRONICLES
. . . and here's a sampling:

Johnny Ringo — lauded as "King of the Cowboys," he turned
up dead as a doornail in very mysterious circumstances.

John Clum — the young New Yorker lived a life of adventure
in Apache country and started the Tombstone newspaper
that still publishes today.

Curly Bill Brocius — a vicious bully with a sense of rhythm,
he set everyone to dancing . . . at gunpoint.

Endicott Peabody — Tombstone's young Episcopal pastor
delivered some well-placed blows for charity.

Read other books in the
WILD WEST COLLECTION,
fast-paced, real-life stories of when the Old West
was still young and rowdy,
where anything could happen — and too often did.

DAYS OF DESTINY
MANHUNTS & MASSACRES
LAW OF THE GUN
THEY LEFT THEIR MARK
STALWART WOMEN (available in 1999)

Turn to the back of this book to read more about them.

Design: MARY WINKELMAN VELGOS
Copy Editor: STEVE FOX
Research: JEB STUART ROSEBROOK
Production: ELLEN STRAINE
Photographic enhancement: VICKY SNOW
Front cover art: DAN MIEDUCH
Back cover art, Map: KEVIN KIBSEY

ABOUT THE COVER:
Take the Money and Run (oil), while not an actual Tombstone scene, depicts
the lawlessness typical of mining towns in the West. The painting also shows
Dan Mieduch's careful study of frontier edifaces, clothing, and firearms. His
delight in such historical detail inspires his hobby of building replicas of
antique American rifles.

ABOUT THE ARTIST:
Dan Mieduch graduated with a degree in Industrial Design from the University
of Michigan and built a successful commercial art career in Detroit before
moving to Phoenix with wife Rhonda. Dan began translating Arizona's wild
beauty and endless horizons into color-drenched oil paintings, selling first in
Scottsdale, Arizona, and then with phenomenal success in Sedona. "In a
painting, it's the feeling, the essence that counts," Dan said. "The mood and
special light of a time of day. The coldness of a snowy night. The heat of a
desert day in summer. Or the boredom of traversing everlasting spaces.
People fall asleep at the wheel . . . just as they fell asleep at the reins in
covered wagon days. That's what I want to convey when I paint."

AUTHORS:
Bob Boze Bell, Chapters 1 and 5; Larry Winter, Chapter 2; Bernard L.
Fontana, Chapter 3; Leo W. Banks, Chapters 4, 6, 7, 9, 10, 11, 15, 16, and 17;
Peter Aleshire, Chapter 8; Cheryl Baisden, Chapter 12; Don Dedera, Chapter
13; Dean Smith, Chapter 14.

Prepared by the Book Division of *Arizona Highways*® magazine, a monthly
publication of the Arizona Department of Transportation.

Publisher — Nina M. La France
Managing Editor — Bob Albano
Associate Editor — Evelyn Howell
Art Director — Mary Winkelman Velgos
Production Director — Cindy Mackey

Printed in the United States
Library of Congress Catalog Number 98-66072
ISBN 0-916179-76-1

TOMBSTONE CHRONICLES

Tough Folks, Wild Times

Authors:
PETER ALESHIRE
CHERYL BAISDEN
LEO W. BANKS
BOB BOZE BELL
DON DEDERA
BERNARD L. FONTANA
DEAN SMITH
LARRY WINTER

Book Editor:
EVELYN HOWELL

CONTENTS

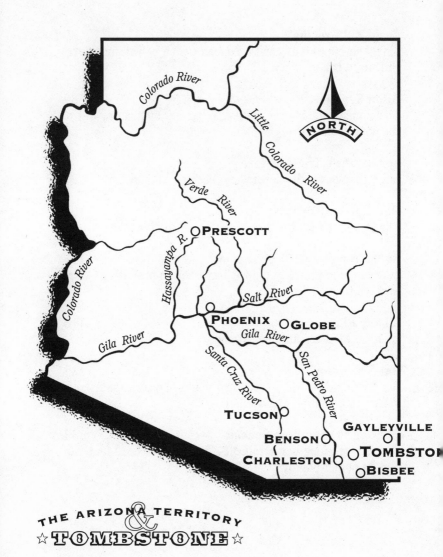

Colorado River

Little Colorado River

NORTH

Verde River

O **PRESCOTT**

Hassayampa R.

Colorado River

Salt River

PHOENIX O **GLOBE**

Gila River

Gila River

San Pedro River

Santa Cruz River

TUCSON O

GAYLEYVILLE
O
BENSON O
TOMBSTON
CHARLESTON O
O **BISBEE**

THE ARIZONA TERRITORY
& ☆ TOMBSTONE ☆

The *town too tough to die* . . . as an icon of the Old West, the Arizona town of Tombstone commands an enthusiastic following, not only of history buffs and scholars, but moviegoers and television fans as well. *Tombstone Chronicles* is a collection of 17 historical profiles representing some of the best and the worst of a brief, exciting time in Tombstone's early life.

As much as it is debated now, that period was perhaps even more controversial for those who lived it. What they knew as truth was determined by personal allegiances as much as by actual circumstance. Every story had at least two sides, if not more, but not every side was told with equal vigor.

The *Arizona Highways* writers who contributed their works for this book have accumulated among them decades of experience in historical research. As these writers already know, perspectives can change with the specific historical sources available. Just the simple spelling of names can be debated: Is it McLaury or McLowery, Claibourn or Claibourne? (Documents from that time show each of these spellings.) Some of these historical variations are apparent throughout this book, highlighting the fact that there is not always a single truth in historical accounts, even eyewitness ones. What may seem contradictory cannot always be assumed to be wrong, especially when the topic is Tombstone.

This book does not pretend to be the whole story. May each chapter, though, whet your appetite to know more about a town where the wild and woolly romped side by side with the sophisticated and cultured.

WHEN TOMBSTONE WAS "BOSS"

*Territorial life had all the grit and grime one
would expect in a desert boomtown,
but it was also surprisingly modern.
For those who managed to survive murder and
mishap, Tombstone provided every luxury.*

BY BOB BOZE BELL

O N THE CHILLY EVENING OF OCTOBER 25, 1881, TOMBSTONE
residents snuggled in and looked forward to a promising morrow. It seemed assured that the city fathers'
ambitious hopes and plans would succeed: Their new metropolis was on the verge of becoming the brightest star between
Kansas City and San Francisco.

The fledgling Arizona town was barely three years old, but
already it had accomplished much to be proud of. Wide, surveyed streets and gas lighting. A mining-exchange building
with a stock market and telephones (with connections to the
main mines). A recently installed water line, making indoor
tubs and toilets a reality in many homes and businesses. The
tennis courts, skating rink, horse-racing track, and hospital
were already built. Plans for a state-of-the-art courthouse, municipal swimming pool, and firehouse were in the works.

In spite of its industrious progress, the Tombstone of
October, 1881, still had the quiet charm of a frontier village.

On October 23, bank clerk and mining man George
Parsons wrote in his diary: "Quiet as usual today. Read up my
papers and ate my bread and bacon with usual composure.

**TOMBSTONE STUDENTS POSED IN FRONT
OF THE PUBLIC SCHOOL, CIRCA 1890.**

Nothing new yet in these parts. Rather monotonous. I hope this state of things won't continue long."

As the vaqueros were fond of saying, "Be careful what you wish for."

Unbeknownst to Parsons and the rest of Tombstone's residents, the events of October 26, 1881, loomed like an iceberg in the night.

The "village" had grown up quickly. In the fall of 1877, scout and prospector Ed Schieffelin filed claims on two mines, the "Toombstone" (his spelling) and "Graveyard," located on a barren, cactus-studded plateau called Goose Flats. By April, 1878, the word was out, and prospectors, swells, cardsharps, ladies of the evening, and adventurers of every stripe began to converge on southeastern Arizona's barren hills, staking claims right and left and, in many cases, literally on top of each other.

By the spring of 1880, big money had arrived. Huge infusions of capital came from San Francisco, Chicago, New York, and even Europe as everyone tried to hit the jackpot by throwing mass quantities of greenbacks all over town.

With the capital came the latest in technology and fashion. Tombstone had more than its share of geologists, engineers, and college professors. And the businesses that sprang up to meet their needs sported the latest in everything.

Bartenders were as adept at mixing sophisticated drinks as they were at drawing beer. Cowboys stood at the bar and asked for gin fizzes, toddies, and champagne. A visitor in 1882 remarked, "The landlord of our hotel described [the cowboys] as 'perfect gentlemen,' some of them good at the bar for as high as $20 or $25 a day."

Kelly's Wine House, one of 66 drinking establishments within the city limits, featured 25 imported wines from Europe, their own microbrewery, a billiards room, bowling alley, and indoor shooting range!

Oyster bars were all the go. Packed in ice, shipments of the ocean delicacies were shipped by rail from San Francisco to Benson, Arizona. From Benson, freight wagons hauled the oysters overland into Tombstone.

Ice cream parlors proliferated. As an old man, Wyatt Earp recalled, "I liked to eat ice cream in Tombstone." His favorite place, the Ice Cream Saloon, was on Fourth Street just around the corner from the O.K. Corral.

There were several competitors. A half-block away, Earl & Banning's shop advertised "ice cold soda water, fresh home-made candy and ice cream." Carleton's Coffee, Oyster, and Chop House at 523 Allen Street served ice cream and everything else in the title.

Not to be outdone, the Gem Coffee and Ice Cream Parlor featured hot chocolate and ice cream. And the Crystal Palace Ice Cream Saloon — not to be confused with the Crystal Palace Bar, which opened in 1882 — offered not only ice cream, but French lunches and wine, as well. Obviously, Tombstone citizens had a pronounced sweet tooth.

Coming into camp from the railhead at Benson, Tombstone-bound travelers boarded a six-horse Concord stage for the dusty 25-mile trip. After lunching and changing horses at Contention, the passengers held on for dear life as the stage climbed out of the San Pedro Valley and snaked across the barren foothills toward a tight row of conical hills. Periodically, the stage moved off to the right of the deep ruts to pass the

FAMED VAUDEVILLE COMEDIAN EDDIE FOY
PERFORMED AT THE BIRD CAGE THEATRE, CIRCA 1885.
THIS PUBLICITY PHOTO WAS PHOTOGRAPHED AT FLY STUDIO.

slower 16-mule-team freight wagons. Mexican drivers walked alongside in the yellow dust and cracked their long "black-snake" bullwhips.

A weary traveler remarked that the scenery was "bare and stoney" and that "on the few wayside fences that exist were painted flaring announcements as 'Go to Bangley and Schlagenstein's At Tombstone. They Are The Bosses. You Bet.'" ("Boss" was a trendy slang word of the day meaning, among other things, "excellent." Judge Wells Spicer referred to Tombstone as "the boss town" in his writings, and later there was a popular eatery called the Boss Restaurant at 605 Allen Street.) As the lathered horses pulled the creaking stagecoach up the last hill, more advertisements could be seen on a huge, circular water tank squatting on a hill on the outskirts of town.

Approaching Tombstone proper, one hopscotched between grubby and grandiose, gritty and glitzy. "The outskirts of Tombstone consisted of huts and tents," wrote a visitor coming in on the stage in 1882. "A burly miner could be seen stretched upon his cot in a windowless cabin, barely large enough to contain him. There were some tents provided with wooden doors and adobe chimneys."

The sounds of carpenters, masons, hod carriers, and laborers hard at work — sawing, hammering, and swearing — filled the air as new buildings went up everywhere. Whistles blew and powder-faced miners came up out of numerous mine shafts literally between buildings.

In the center of town, a row of sturdy commercial buildings bristled. The brand-new Cosmopolitan Hotel, a 50-room, two-story building, furnished its rooms with bedroom sets of black walnut and rosewood.

Loungers and bums lined the streets, waiting for the stage and the opportunity to see the new faces that arrived twice a day. Some of those new faces might end up in the makeshift jail, a 10-by-12-foot wooden slat (flat side up) affair with one door and no windows, which was used when there wasn't room to keep prisoners at the San Jose House.

Newcomers complained about the high prices. A "good" meal could run as high as 50 cents. A gallon of whiskey ran $2 to $8. A lamp cost $6. A shanty that cost $50 to build rented for $15 a month. A pillow cost $1.

A travel writer called Tombstone "that aggressive spasm of modernism." No one haggled over price, he complained: "The most expensive of everything is what is most wanted."

Most of the merchants were there for the easy money. As one wife put it, "This is a place to stay in for a while: not a desirable spot for a permanent home."

The explosion of growth was staggering. In March, 1879, Tombstone's population stood at 250, with a dozen new arrivals every week. By September, the number of residents passed 500, and by the end of the year, it was pushing 1,000.

TOMBSTONE AND BISBEE BASEBALL TEAMS, CIRCA 1895.

By February, 1880, the population had swelled to 2,000, with 20 new arrivals every day. On the evening of October 25, 1881, some 4,000 residents called Tombstone home. One thing became crystal clear early on: Tombstone needed to get its act together.

Led by a local justice of the peace, the Tombstone Town Site Company was formed to establish proper title to the town's lots. The company approached building owners and offered to sell them clear title to their property. The sore spot in the deal was that the price of clear title depended on the value of property improvements, meaning that the more substantial the building owner's investment, the more the owner had to pay.

Although the company's paper had a quasi-legal basis, essentially, the Town Site Company was selling the property back to the landowners. And, although the company was officially sanctioned by Mayor Alder Randall and the town council, many in the fledgling community refused to pay. There were rumors of hired thugs trying to strong-arm the footdraggers. The ensuing scandal immediately divided Tombstone

A TOMBSTONE PROSPECTOR AND HIS MULE OUTFIT.

along partisan lines and set the stage for subsequent events.

The wife of a mining engineer, Clara Spalding Brown came to Tombstone to keep house and to serve as a correspondent for the *San Diego Union*.

On July 7, 1880, in her first dispatch, she wrote: "It is a place more pretentious than I had imagined, and full of activity, notwithstanding the hundreds of loungers seen upon the streets. The only attractive places visible are the liquor and gambling saloons, which are everywhere present and are carpeted and comfortably furnished.

"The ladies of Tombstone are not so liberally provided with entertainment, and find little enjoyment aside from a stroll about town after sunset, the only comfortable time of the day. The camp is one of the dirtiest places in the world . . . and one is never sure of having a clean face, despite repeated ablutions. It is time to talk about dirt. The sod lies loose upon the surface, and is whirled into the air every day by a wind which almost amounts to a gale; it makes the eyes smart like the cinders from an engine: it penetrates into the houses, and covers everything with dust."

As for churches, Mrs. Brown wrote: "Religious services are held in a furniture store, and attended by the few who know when Sunday comes around."

While Tombstone made sure it got its share of imported wine and oysters, other amenities were hard to come by: "We cannot obtain desirable food for hot weather; fresh vegetables are scarce, and the few fruits in the markets require a very large purse," Mrs. Brown noted.

By 1881, Tombstone was Arizona Territory's second largest city (behind Tucson), and the feisty newcomer already had two daily newspapers!

The first newspaper was the *Tombstone Nugget*, which published its first issue on October 2, 1879. Legend says that Ed Schieffelin named the other — Tombstone's most famous newspaper. The story goes that he was riding into the district on a stage with John Clum, who, it is said, asked the passengers to suggest a name for the paper he was about to start.

"The Epitaph," Schieffelin said without taking a breath. "That's the name for a paper that will celebrate in enduring print the deeds and fame of Tombstone."

Clum wasn't convinced: "But epitaphs are usually mere chiseled lies."

"Well," Schieffelin deadpanned, "they tell the truth about as often as newspapers."

The cowboys and ranchers of newly formed Cochise County were predominately Democrats of Southern origin, and their voice was the *Nugget*, while the bulk of the businessmen (including the Earps) of Tombstone were Republicans, and Yankee sympathizers. The *Epitaph* championed their causes.

There were two tiers of entertainment in Tombstone. Most of the saloons and gambling establishments catered to the rough crowd — the cowboys, miners, and working classes — with games of keno, faro, and poker, spiced with scantily clad dancing women and bawdy displays.

However, for the more refined there were Shakespearean plays, performances of Gilbert and Sullivan's *H.M.S. Pinafore*, and costume parties, such as the Martha Washington Tea Party, given at Schieffelin Hall. For this elite, invitation-only party, colonial costumes were ordered from San Francisco, powdered wigs were worn by the men, and a very elegant minuet was danced by numerous preening couples.

The Grand Hotel, the Russ House, and the Rockaway Oyster House offered gourmet dinners. Nellie Cashman, the camp angel, operated the Russ House, and for Thanksgiving, 1881, she served salmon, corned beef, ham, veal cutlets, fillet, ox tongue, and homemade pies, cakes, and puddings. All for 50 cents.

Soiled doves and their cribs were confined to a block on East Allen Street, although cyprians (one of the many names for frontier prostitutes) could be seen in almost all of the gambling dens.

Tombstone and nearby Charleston fielded baseball teams and played each other on holidays. Whist clubs, French clubs, and glee clubs abounded.

As for ailments in the camp, one wag put it this way: "Whiskey and cold lead are named as the leading diseases at Tombstone." But in spite of Tombstone's reputation as having "a man for breakfast every morning," there is some controversy as to the extent of violence in the infamous boomtown. Clara Brown was mildly surprised at the lack of violence when she reported, "Only one killing since we've been here."

On the other hand, a visitor from back East noted, "To kill your man seems a way of winning your spurs, as it were, and establishing yourself on a proper footing in the community."

Considering that most men in the camp went armed and that almost as many were drunk, it's probably a miracle that the number of killings was so low (only five in a two-year period). Wyatt Earp himself seemed to echo that sentiment. In a deposition for an estate case in 1925, Earp was asked if Tombstone had been bad, and the old lawman promptly replied, "Not half as bad as L.A."

Nonetheless, the violence that did occur was quite dramatic and created sensational headlines across the nation. Also, it must be noted that there were many killings outside the

RANCHER JOHN SLAUGHTER ALSO HELPED
CLEAN UP TOMBSTONE AS COCHISE COUNTY SHERIFF.
THIS PORTRAIT, CIRCA 1888, WAS PHOTOGRAPHED
AT FLY STUDIO.

city limits. Parsons, at one point in early 1882, counted 14 killings in 10 days.

Riding herd on violence within the city limits was Virgil Earp, the capable and no-nonsense city marshal. From time to time, he was assisted by his brothers, Wyatt and Morgan.

The Earps were not the only lawmen to serve Cochise County with distinction. Former Texan John Slaughter was a powerful force along the border, literally settling right on the boundary line with Mexico and daring his enemies to unseat him. They tried many times, but never succeeded. Later, Slaughter served as sheriff of Cochise County and cleaned out his share of bad men before retiring.

Other notable fighting men rode the ranges of southern Arizona, and their exploits sent Tombstone's fame "swirling to the frontier skies in clouds of six-shooter smoke." Among them: Buckskin Frank Leslie, Luke Short, Curly Bill Brocius, Johnny Ringo, Pony Deal, Russian Bill, Jaw Bone Clark, Black Jack Ketchum, Bat Masterson, Billy "the Kid" Claiborne, Texas Jack Vermillion, Turkey Creek Johnson, Charlie Storms, and Zwing Hunt. Quite a list for quite a town.

For the first several decades of its existence, Tombstone was constantly in turmoil and transition. Booming, busting, and burning down (two times in two years). On May 26, 1886, a pump shaft burned, flooding the mines. Later, newer, more powerful pumps were brought in to pump the water out.

Upsizing, downsizing, Tombstone came close to dying more than once. (During the mid-1890s, many of Tombstone's buildings were hauled off to Pearce, a rival boomtown which boomed, flourished, and quickly died.) But somehow Tombstone managed to survive every calamity and downturn, ultimately earning for itself the feisty slogan: the town too tough to die.

Yes, it was a hopeful, chilly night on the evening of October 25, 1881, out on the modern, industrialist frontier. Tombstone's defining moment and enduring legacy in the annals of the Wild West was yet to come. As the Grand Hotel's big clock slowly ticked towards midnight, it is safe to assume that virtually none of the ambitious residents of Arizona's newest and brightest mining mecca had a clue about what that legacy would be.

CHAPTER TWO

THE SCHIEFFELIN BROTHERS & DICK GIRD

Ed Schieffelin struggled for years for that one fantastic strike. What he discovered in southeastern Arizona transformed him and his partners into rich men, but Ed still wanted something more than mere wealth.

BY LARRY WINTER

———◆◆◆———

"IT IS MY WISH," ED SCHIEFFELIN WROTE IN HIS WILL, "to be buried in the garb of a prospector, my old pick and canteen with me, about three miles westerly from the town of Tombstone . . . at my first camp near the mines I discovered."

The man who uncovered the Tombstone silver lode still rests within it, buried as he directed beneath a pile of stones like "prospectors build when locating a mining claim." Even today, the site is dry, lonely, desolate. Only a visionary or a very lucky, very stubborn, very desperate man could have seen the spot for what it was: cubic foot by cubic foot, the richest ground ever mined in America.

Other prospectors had probed the then-nameless Tombstone Hills, then hurried west to the more inviting San Pedro Valley.

The hills were dangerous, to be sure — Cochise's stronghold in the Dragoon Mountains was less than 10 miles away, and cutthroats routinely ambushed honest pioneers — but fear alone didn't stop the old-timers.

Mostly, the place looked bad. What meager ore that did surface was unpromising. Apparently filled with lead, it offered no hint of the thick silver veins running for thousands of feet beneath the desert floor.

Schieffelin was nearly 30 when he entered Arizona in January, 1877. He had just finished a fruitless, 18-year prospect through Oregon, California, Utah, and Idaho. His earliest adventure was typical.

ED SCHIEFFELIN,
PHOTOGRAPHED BY
MOLLIE FLY, CIRCA 1882.

"The first thing I did," he remembered, "was to get a shovel and a milk pail, and to go down to the bank of the river looking for gold. That was my first experience with mica." For a long time, it was the only mineral he could find.

He chased strikes from Greenhorn Canyon to Poker Flat to Puke Ravine but always arrived at the tail end of the boom times. Yet by 1877, Schieffelin had accumulated a respectable grubstake, two healthy mules, a fine rifle, and plenty of ammunition.

And he had an attitude.

"I determined," he wrote later, "I would follow no more excitements and pay no attention to anything that anybody else had found, but I would try something of my own, and I did so."

Holding true to this determination, in Territorial Arizona he found places no white man had seen, much less prospected.

Early in 1877, Schieffelin explored the Grand Canyon, but its ancient seafloors held only fossils. Soon he joined a party of Hualapai Indians heading southeast to scout for the

Cavalry. Some Hualapais claimed that treasure lay hidden in the rock of the southern mountains. At least the region passed Schieffelin's main test: It was unexplored, thanks to the Apaches.

Camp Huachuca had just been founded on the western edge of the San Pedro Valley. From there, Schieffelin accompanied the Hualapais on their frequent scouting expeditions, but soon he struck out on his own.

Occasionally, he returned to Camp Huachuca to restock his supplies.

In his favorite version of the origin of the name "Tombstone" (but not his only one), Schieffelin claimed that soldiers once asked him what he sought in the hills. "Stones," Schieffelin replied. "Ha," they snorted. "The only stone you will find there is your tombstone."

In time, he found what he took to be ore and loaded his mules down with it. Flat broke, he could not afford to file a claim, so he interested a wrangler named Griffith in a partnership. They rode into Tucson to stake a claim and find backers, but many local speculators had recently learned expensive lessons about grubstakes. Since there was no assayer in Tucson, the ore couldn't be fairly evaluated, and every self-proclaimed expert pronounced the samples worthless.

James McClintock, an early historian, described Schieffelin during this visit as ". . . about the queerest specimen of humanity ever seen in Tucson. His clothing was worn and covered with patches of deerskins, corduroy and flannel, and his old slouch hat too, was so pieced with rabbit skin that very little of the original felt remained. Although only twenty-nine years of age he looked at least forty."

Discouraged, Griffith gave up prospecting. Schieffelin, however, decided to go back. Whatever anyone said, he believed the rock was good. He made preparations and, with 30 cents in his pocket, headed north to find his brother, Al.

At Globe, he looked for Al in the mines nearby. But Al had long since gone to the McCracken Mine outside Signal

City in the far northwest of Arizona Territory.

Thoroughly broke, Ed Schieffelin landed the meanest job in the Territory: night operator of the hoist at a two-bit silver mine. Dressed in skins, in the cold darkness, and without a fire, he hauled up a dozen tons of ore every night by cranking a hand windlass.

When he had earned enough, he left for Signal City and finally found Al. Then he found Richard Gird. Gird, already famous in the Territory as an Indian fighter, mapmaker, and incomparable mining engineer, had just taken the post of assayer at the McCracken Mine and was slated for superintendent.

When Gird finished assaying Ed's samples, his findings stunned the Schieffelins, even Ed. The best sample assayed at $2,000 a ton, 20 times richer than the McCracken ore, at that time the Territory's richest.

Immediately, Gird proposed a partnership, abandoning the certainties of position to partner with the Schieffelins. He knew them well enough, especially Al, whom Gird called "honest, truthful and naturally good." Ed was boastful, proud, self-conscious, but like his brother, fundamentally "honorable and true." Gird provided a mule, a wagon, his assay outfit, his experience, connections, and savvy.

Gird had spent the past 20 years alternately chasing chances like this — in 1873, he nearly discovered the McCracken Mine himself, but stopped one valley too far north. Gird knew Ed's strike was a long shot; prospectors sometimes struck small pockets of unbelievably rich ore that played out in a week. But Gird was 41 in a land that was hard on even young men. This might be his last prospect.

At 16, in 1851, he had started on his first prospect when he left his father's dairy farm in Herkimer County, New York, to meet his brother, Henry, in California. There he had prospected for gold, but along the way had also learned assaying, metallurgy, and mining.

After seven years, Gird went backpacking through Chile, hoping for work in the copper mines. Instead, he stayed to

survey railroad lines for the legendary railroad man Harry Meigs.

Engineering and mechanics
had come easily to him. As a boy,
he studied surveying, chemistry,
and trigonometry at the country
school near his father's farm.

When he arrived in Arizona
in 1861, Gird brought the first
civil-engineering and surveying
outfit seen in the Territory. Within
two years, he had helped William
D. Bradshaw build a ferry across

RICHARD GIRD

the Colorado River where Ehrenberg now stands, opening central Arizona to traffic with California. Later, Bradshaw and
Gird broke the first trail from the Colorado across the desert to
the site of Prescott. Other pioneers called it "Gird's Road."

Like Ed, Gird learned some bitter lessons on the frontier. In 1863, he led a party of 13 into Apacheria to prospect for
gold and silver. These were hard men, prepared to fight every
foot of the way, but within the year, all but three or four of
Gird's companions had been killed by Indians.

Later in 1864, Gird joined King Woolsey's third militia
expedition against the Apaches. One of Arizona Territory's early
entrepreneurs, Woolsey was a mine developer, rancher, mill
owner, and stage operator. He also made time to fight a cold-
blooded war against the native tribes. Receiving no quarter
from the Apaches, he gave no quarter himself, even supposedly offering poisoned corn to Indians at a peace parley and killing
Indian women and children rather than capturing them.

Woolsey's militia expeditions of the 1860s were meant to
defend the early mining camps of central Arizona Territory from
Indian attacks, but the fallout from his brutal tactics helped
provoke more warfare. The war between the United States
Army and the Tonto Apaches would not end until General George
Crook defeated the Tonto Apaches in the mid-1870s.

By Woolsey's third expedition, the Apaches recognized the futility of open battle with whites and chose ambush instead. For the better part of a year, Woolsey's 100 men ranged from Prescott to the Gila River, allowing Gird to prospect whole new lands. Everywhere he went, Gird systematically surveyed the surrounding country.

In 1865, he drew the first official map of Arizona for the Territorial Legislature. His map shows a "route of exploration" from Bradshaw's Ferry to the Castle Domes Mines, east through the Eagle Tail Mountains and south of the Harquahala Mountains into Wickenburg. The map also charts a "Wagon Road Discovered by Gird and Sage, November 1863."

Now it was January, 1878, and Gird was partner with the Schieffelins. Snow covered northern Arizona, and Gird suggested they travel in the spring. But Ed, obsessed by the mines he knew lay in the south, forced them to leave as soon as possible, February 14.

Storms dogged them from Mohave County to Wickenburg, to Hayden's Ferry on the Salt River. There they had joined the Overland Stage route, then steered south for Tucson. In the dimly known regions Gird and the Schieffelins crossed after they left Tucson in 1878, they could depend on no one but themselves.

Many years later, Ed Schieffelin described Gird and himself as "hard men." He meant they could go without water, work in the sun, hold up their end, learn a lesson, and not complain. Gird was private, dour. According to the pioneering Cochise County rancher J. A. Rockfellow, Gird was "a man without a shred of self-importance." He inspired great loyalty. Many men followed him from one job to another

From Tucson the trio headed east, entered Apache lands, then turned south into the valley of the San Pedro, which they reached in March. At first, they could not trace the complicated geology leading from the ore Ed had found a year earlier to its source in the mother lode.

Then the Schieffelin brothers rode out to hunt deer one

morning, and Ed broke off to prospect. All day he traced fragments of ore across country, but in a new direction, up and to the north. He found a vein of silver so soft and rich that when he swung his pick at the ore, it sunk in all the way up to the shaft. When he pressed a coin into the ore, the coin left behind a clear impression of its face. He called the strike the "Lucky Cuss." The ore assayed at $15,000 a ton.

Other, bigger strikes soon followed, such as Tough Nut and Grand Central. Other prospectors came, drawn by Gird's reputation. He assayed ore for some of the newcomers with the clear understanding that he and the Schieffelins would share in any discoveries made. As always, these agreements were settled with a handshake.

One prospector, Hank Williams, tried to squirm out of such an agreement, but when Gird, the Schieffelins, and the growing community of local prospectors insisted, Williams reluctantly conceded half of his claim to the other three. They named it the Contention.

By April, they were so strapped for cash that they sold their share in the Contention for $10,000. It would later prove to be the richest single claim of all, but at the time, the Contention was just one more promising strike. The $10,000 was merely a fraction of what it would cost to fully exploit their remaining claims.

The Schieffelins, who had never made more than $4 a day, would almost certainly have sold out for a pittance then and there, but Gird knew how to organize a mining district. Under his direction, a shaft was sunk at the Tough Nut, and the first incarnation of Tombstone rose near the site. Gird was elected mayor in December, 1878, and also served as postmaster.

With a steady hand, he ruled the hard cases who began to migrate to the town. Since there was little formal law to aid him, Gird obeyed the true law of the frontier and gathered around him men he could trust. Years later, James Wolf described them: "Gird and many of his early assistants came from the old McCracken Mine. . . . Through many years, all

ED SCHIEFFELIN IN A GROUP SHOT TITLED
"ALASKA PROSPECTING PARTY,"
PHOTOGRAPHED AT FLY STUDIO, CIRCA 1888.

had survived the onslaughts of the mighty Mohave Indian tribes and were dead shots with pistol and rifle, in addition to being fine miners."

Few social conventions had been established to guide behavior, and fewer still were observed. James Wolf and others reported that murder and robbery were common. Rustling enjoyed the status of a robust sport. Men like Gird formed a kind of voluntary order, an order based on mutual respect and loyalty rather than on institutional coercion. The rules were simple: Keep your word, hold up your end, look out for your partner.

By 1879, two corporations had been capitalized: the Corbin Mining and Milling Company, based on the Lucky Cuss and related claims, and the Tombstone Mining and Milling Company, which was founded on the Tough Nut. Gird drove a hard bargain for himself and the Schieffelins. In the end, Gird and the Schieffelins each owned a quarter of both companies, and financiers shared the rest.

With the new capital, Gird sank more shafts, dammed the San Pedro River, and built a pair of ore-reduction mills across the river from the new town of Charleston. In August, 1881, crushing 45 tons of rock a day, the mills produced a record $151,279.15 in silver bullion.

By then, the Schieffelins were gone from Tombstone. They had sold out in 1880 for $300,000 apiece, an act that momentarily strapped Gird, but one he understood. The brothers, especially Ed, were dyed-in-the-wool prospectors, men used to living free and unwashed.

"I was a little dissatisfied with the results of our labor," Ed explained, "and did not think we had accomplished much."

Now Ed could prospect wherever he chose. His sense for treasure proved sharp but untimely. In the spring of 1882, intuition sent him to the Yukon — 15 years before the big gold rush there — but the snow turned him back.

He and some partners went back the next year with a stern-wheeler built especially for travel on the Yukon River. Although they found some coarse gold, and Schieffelin was prepared to stay two years, the shortness of the season depressed his partners. By fall, Ed was back in San Francisco.

Next he tried a prospect of a different sort. In La Junta, Colorado, he married Mary Brown, a widow he'd met in San Francisco. They moved to Los Angeles, and brother Al lived with them.

Gird hung on in Tombstone for another year, eventually cashing in for an amount estimated between $600,000 and $2 million. Before he left, Gird squared up with the Schieffelins. In 1878, the three had sworn to share equally in all matters concerning Tombstone. Now he had sold out for twice what his partners had gotten, and the disparity rankled him. He sent a check to the Schieffelins for the difference, much more than $200,000.

A longtime bachelor, Gird had recently married Nellie McCarty of York, Maine, and San Francisco. In 1882, they bought the Rancho Santa Ana del Chino, a spread of 45,000 acres in Southern California.

Using their own funds, the Girds planned and founded the town of Chino, California, built schools, hired teachers, and developed a system of irrigation based on artesian wells Gird had discovered. They built a narrow gauge railroad to connect Chino to the city of Ontario, then brought families to their land. To give these settlers work, Gird developed the sugar-beet industry in California. In 1910, Gird died peacefully in Chino, having outlived both Schieffelin brothers.

Al Schieffelin had died of consumption in 1885, his lungs broken by a life of toil in dusty mines. He had enjoyed his fortune for a scant five years.

Ed lived another 12 years, leaving no heirs besides his wife and another brother. "I have no children," he noted in his will, "but should anyone at their own expense, prove to the satisfaction of my executors to be a child of mine, to each I give the sum of $50."

With his affairs settled, he went prospecting. He spent his last year in a primitive cabin high in the Oregon Cascades. He searched for gold he didn't need or even crave. He just wanted to touch the mother lode one more time.

Less than half a year short of his 50th birthday, he did. But he never shared the secret.

Schieffelin died in May, 1896, while cracking ore samples in his cabin. He was found alone, body slumped peacefully across a worktable, his belongings untouched. The coroner quickly ruled out suicide and foul play, but the assayer's report proved more dramatic: When tested, Schieffelin's last sack of ore samples came in at more than $2,000 to the ton.

But Ed Schieffelin left behind neither map nor directions to his discovery. Others could find the treasure on their own; Schieffelin had what he wanted. The last entry in his journal read simply, "Struck it rich again, by God."

CHAPTER THREE

JOHN CLUM

Audacious and ambitious, John P. Clum found
adventure of many kinds when he came out
West. From Indian agent with the Apaches to
newspaper publisher and Tombstone's mayor,
he made an enduring name for himself.

BY BERNARD L. FONTANA

⟨❖⟩

FOR JOHN P. CLUM — INDIAN AGENT, NEWSPAPER PUBLISHER, and politician — audacity was a way of life. He may be best remembered for founding the *Tombstone Epitaph* newspaper and being Tombstone's mayor during the Earp days, but even his early career shows a man who made bold, decisive moves.

Born September 1, 1851, on a farm in New York's Hudson River Valley, Clum was not obviously destined for the Wild West. He was a second-year divinity student at Rutgers College when illness forced him to drop out. While recuperating, however, he learned that the Army Signal Service was setting up weather observation stations in New Mexico, and he enlisted.

From September, 1871, to January, 1874, while serving in Santa Fe, he became a founder of the local Young Men's Christian Association and befriended Territorial Governor Marsh Giddings. Clum and the politician became so close that Clum lived for three months in Giddings' suite at the Palace of Governors while the governor was away on business.

Clum might have stayed in Santa Fe had not the Dutch Reformed Church nominated him as an Indian agent, a federal job that paid the handsome annual stipend of $1,600. (After 1870, Indian agents were nominated to their posts by Christian religious denominations.) In August, 1874, Clum found himself at the San Carlos Indian Agency in Arizona Territory.

Just six months earlier, the Apaches had surrendered to Army troops after having, in the words of First Lt. J. B. Babcock, "committed sundry acts of violence upon citizens of the United States." In a letter to Clum, Babcock wrote that the Indians, who had been hiding in the mountains, "were pursued by the Military forces and punished. . . . They came in, band by band, and surrendered to me."

Clum, a stocky 5 feet 8 inches tall, became an instant expert on the Apaches. Two days after he assumed his post, he held a council with the "Chiefs of the Tribes" — presumably band headmen — and announced himself "pleased with their deportment and conversation."

He told the men he would inspect their villages about sunset. In a report to the commissioner of Indian affairs, Clum said: "I was warmly greeted by the chiefs and warriors of each band. The men, women, and children were formed in line for inspection and count [about 800 of them]. Their houses [built of brush] were very neat and clean, and every observation impressed me in a most favorable manner. I think they are far more intelligent than any other tribe I ever met. . . . I trust that your Department will lose no time in furnishing this Agency such funds and implements etc. as I shall immediately recommend which are vital to the prosperity of these Indians and the success of the Agency."

Clum also deemed that the success of the agency and "his" Indians depended on his maintaining absolute jurisdiction over their affairs. He decided the best rule was self-rule, and he took the unprecedented step — in the Southwest, at least — of organizing an Apache court and police force, institutions which are echoed in today's federal policy of Indian self-determination. He instructed the U.S. military that its only responsibility on the reservation was by his invitation.

Before long the people at San Carlos called Clum *Nantan-betunnykahyeh*, "Boss with the high forehead," a reference to his rapidly receding hair-line. During his three years as Indian agent at San Carlos, Clum earned the respect of most of the Western Apaches among whom he lived and for whom he had genuine respect and affection.

JOHN P. CLUM

Clum formed a road show consisting of 22 San Carlos Apaches. Billed as "Wild Apaches," in 1876 they went on tour. The St. Louis performance, the only one given, was less than successful financially, and it appeared that Clum would have trouble repaying the $3,000 he borrowed for the journey. But the commissioner of Indian affairs was persuaded to cover the cost of their return trip. Clum accompanied his troupe back as far as El Moro, Colorado. There he left them and headed — at government expense — to Delaware, Ohio, to wed Mary Dennison Ware.

When and where Clum had met Mary Ware is unclear. She was the niece of William Dennison, onetime governor of Ohio, chairman of the Republican convention that nominated Abraham Lincoln, and a former postmaster general. Clum had proposed to Mary by mail, and she had accepted. They were married on November 8, 1876, and honeymooned in San Francisco before taking up residence at San Carlos on January 1, 1877.

Accepted as he was by the Western Apaches, Clum was not popular among the Chiricahua Apaches. In 1876, he was required to bring in all the Chiricahuas who were living in southeastern Arizona after the revocation of an 1872 executive order establishing their reservation.

And, in 1877, Clum's men had captured Geronimo, a Chiricahua leader, in New Mexico and brought him to San Carlos as a prisoner. Clum later touted this event as "the only capture" of Geronimo, but Geronimo pointed out that Clum's achievement was based on a ruse, taunting his enemies that "you never caught me shooting."

If the Chiricahuas disliked Clum, the U.S. military establishment liked him even less. Since its creation in 1849, the Department of the Interior had been responsible for managing Indian affairs. But on the frontier, management was often left in the hands of the War Department. Army personnel accused civilian agents of coddling Indians, while Army supporters in Congress and among journalists decried the "mawkish sentimentality" of Indian agents.

Clum fought a verbal and written war with the military in personal and official correspondence and in the newspapers. In 1877, the Interior Department rejected his public offer to "assume responsibility for all Apaches in Arizona." He then let it be known that he would not submit to an inspection of his agency or its Indians by the Army, and, when his notice was ignored, he quit.

On July 1, 1877, he packed his bags, never again to serve in the role of Indian agent. John and Mary Clum moved to Tucson, where he studied law and where, in 1878, their son, Woodworth, was born.

They next moved to the town of Florence, and Clum became an attorney. He bought the *Arizona Citizen* from his friend, John Wasson, and published the newspaper in Florence for a year before moving it back to Tucson. In February, 1879, it became the first daily to be published in Arizona. The present *Tucson Citizen* is its direct descendant.

Then came Tombstone's silver strike. Alert to the opportunities, Clum sold the *Citizen* and moved his young family to Tombstone in April, 1880.

Clum, Billy Breakenridge, and the brothers Earp converged on the new mining settlement soon after it changed from a disorganized frontier camp to a genuine village. Incorporated in December, 1879, Tombstone needed a justice of the peace court, town ordinances, and a marshal.

Like the Earps, Clum was a staunch Republican, and his newly founded newspaper, the *Tombstone Epitaph,* reflected those political sentiments from its first issue, published in May, 1880. He supported Republicans, among them Wyatt Earp, for public offices.

He also dueled editorially with the *Tombstone Nugget,* the rival Democratic newspaper, whose principals were active in Territorial government in Prescott and Pima County. The *Nugget* was inclined to support the "cowboy faction" of Tombstone, men who tended to be Southern Democrats and whom Clum referred to as the "cowboy curse."

In December, 1880, Mary Clum died giving birth to a daughter. The infant died a few days later, and the bereaved father was forced to send his young son to live with relatives in the East.

The next month, less than three weeks after Mary's death, Clum beat his Democratic opponent in the race for mayor of Tombstone by an overwhelming vote of 532-165. He also served as chairman of the board of school trustees in 1880-81 and was twice Tombstone's postmaster, once in 1880-82 and again in 1884-86.

During the interim, he went to Washington, D.C., to serve as clerk in the office of the chief inspector of the Post Office Department. He married Belle Atwood and fathered a daughter, Caro Kingsland Clum.

In the sharply factionalized political terrain of Tombstone, not everyone agreed with Clum's views. For example, while some would characterize Wyatt Earp as "notorious," Clum regarded him as "my ideal of the strong, manly, serious and capable peace officer." He remained firm in this conviction even after the infamous 1881 O.K. Corral shoot-out.

No favorite of Clum was Territorial Governor John Frémont. Despite being a fellow Republican, Frémont appointed Democrat Johnny Behan as sheriff, rather than the celebrated Wyatt Earp . Frémont, Clum charged in an editorial, had made "a bargain with the Democrats, giving them the control [of Cochise County]. The Republicans, by virtue of a 250 majority in the whole of the county's last election, were at least entitled to a share of the offices."

In May, 1886, during Clum's second Tombstone sojourn, a fire destroyed Tombstone's Grand Central pump house and hoisting works, a disaster from which the mines never recovered. Clum and his new family left for California that same year. After a varied career that took him throughout the United States and to Alaska, and after a third marriage following Belle's death in 1912, he returned to Tombstone in 1929. There he was present to kick off the town's first annual "Helldorado" celebration.

In 1931, he visited the San Carlos reservation, where he reminisced with elderly Apaches. His granddaughter, Marjorie Clum Parker, tells the story:

> John P. Clum looked quickly at the Apaches and started with a slow, halting step toward the long-anticipated reunion. At the same instant an old Indian, wrinkled, gray, but erect, stepped out from his companions, waved his cane, and came forward gesticulating.
>
> "Nantan-betunnykahyeh," he shouted feebly. . . .
>
> Grandfather hurried. His lips moved but no sound came from them. The two old fellows met. . . . For a moment, they stood in silent embrace — John P. Clum and Goodah-Goodah, one of the original Apache police. . . .
>
> A dust cloud appeared a half a mile up the road. An ancient Indian pony was heading our way, half-walking, half-trotting. . . .

Sneezer, riding bareback, whacked his heels against the pony's ribs, finally slid off, and finished the journey on his own unsteady legs. Half blind but smiling, Sneezer shouted something in Apache. Father [sic] looked quickly at the interpreter, "What did he say?"

"He said pony too slow."

Again two old comrades met, over a lapse of 50 years — again the embrace, a glimpse of tears.

There was a luncheon and an hour-long 'smoke' in the semicircle of red men and one white. Young Apaches stood around on the edges listening. When the goodbyes came at last, Sneezer, dry-eyed but very serious, spoke.

"We will never see you again, Nantan Clum. We are both old men. We have lived long and seen much. Goodbye."

On May 2, 1932, Clum was picking a rose in the garden of his Southern California home when he died of a heart attack.

The memory of his audacious life was not lost, however. In 1936, Woodworth Clum completed the book, *Apache Agent*, an autobiography that his father had started. Hollywood turned the book into the 1956 movie, *Walk the Proud Land*, starring World War II hero Audie Murphy as John Clum.

GEORGE PARSONS

Rats, fires, shoot-outs, lightning strikes — what
George Parsons described in his diary was
the day-to-day truth of early Tombstone.
He saw it all and lived to tell about it.

B Y   L E O   W .   B A N K S

W HEN GEORGE WHITWELL PARSONS JOINED TOMBSTONE'S silver rush, he wanted to strike it rich. It never occurred to him, stepping down from the stagecoach onto Allen Street on February 17, 1880, that he would make his name, not as a rich man, but as an eyewitness.

The day after his arrival, he wrote in his diary: "About 2,000 people claimed for Tombstone. Very lively camp. Fine broad street. Good restaurants. Good square meal four bits. . . . Six shooters part of a man's dress here. Saw Schieffelin original discoverer of Tombstone today. Rough looking customer."

For the next seven years, Parsons' ink scrawl filled numerous small notebooks in that same clipped style, creating for later readers a staccato rattle of observations, gripes, small pleasures, humorous asides and a fair dose of moral preening.

Parsons wrote every day, and although his entries are sometimes maddeningly undetailed — "Several Tombstoners killed by Indians recently" — he was a dogged observer.

He noted everything, from his own money troubles and health woes (backaches and boils) to the camp's progress in getting mail and telegraph lines to the bloody passions that played out on the streets and saloons, leaving "men killed, shot, stabbed, suiciding, etc. every day or two."

And, of course, he watched, and commented on, the relationship between the Earps and the cowboy-outlaws as it sizzled to the fight near the O.K. Corral and its aftermath.

Parsons' voice was but a whisper in those days. After all, these were private writings never intended for wide circulation.

But since his death in 1933, at 82, and the transcription of a portion of his diaries in 1939, this largely forgotten man has become one of history's loudest voices to those seeking the eyewitness truth of Tombstone.

Parsons was born in Washington, D.C., but spent his boyhood in Brooklyn. He was a lifelong bachelor, civic-minded, soulful, a scold to those he deemed unfit. He'd lost his job as a bank teller in San Francisco when talk of the Tombstone boom captured him. He had to go.

But he was unprepared for frontier living. He spent many of his early nights nearly freezing, sleeping on the dirt floor of a two-room house he shared with three other men.

"Rats and mice made a deuce of a racket last night around a fellow's head on ground. Rolled over on one in the night and killed him — mashed him deader than a door nail."

He wrote about the ceaseless wind, the strangling dust, the solitude, and the gall of an entrepreneur trying to charge $3 a day to rent a horse to ride to nearby Charleston. Parsons walked instead, a 20-mile round-trip. Money was scarce. "Less than $10 on hand," he wrote. "What do I care tho', Let her rip."

Later, as the owner of a mining company and a mill in the Huachuca Mountains, Parsons became a prominent citizen. But he never got rich and never forgot the backbreaking labor of swinging a miner's pick: "My poor hands and arms are in terrible state . . . I've roughed it before — worked hard and endured much physically — but this beats all."

Parsons was a deeply spiritual man. In one entry, he clucked his tongue at the sight of "loose women" leaving church and heading straight to the saloon. In another day's entry, he

**THIS EARLY PHOTOGRAPH
OF GEORGE PARSONS SOMETIMES HAS BEEN
MISIDENTIFIED AS JOHN CLUM.**

commented, "How men of good family and connections east can come here and marry prostitutes — take them out of a dance house — I can't see."

To Parsons' mind, Tombstone seemed accommodating only to floozies. But he did meet a charmer by the name of Miss Colby, and by the sound of it, she made his mustache curl: "She is very pretty and agreeable and a godsend to this forlorn community." He went on to hope that the "fair and virtuous" would replace "those of a coarse, depraved nature who have been so long desporting themselves before the community."

But most of the "desporters" were men, and they performed their desporting chores faithfully, usually with whiskey and revolvers. Parsons commented on them often, such as this entry written his first day in town:

"Shooting this A.M. and two fellows in the afternoon tried to go for one another with guns and six shooters — but friends interposed. No law other than miner's and that doesn't sit and deliberate but acts at once. . . . Everyone goes heeled."

Comments of a similar vein continued over the months. On August 9, 1880: "Seems . . . there are about 25 men in town who wouldn't hesitate to cut a man's throat for $2.50."

On August 25, 1880: "The death roll since I came here, I mean violent deaths, shootings, and poisonings, foots up fearfully large . . . Lynch law is very effective at times — in a community like this."

By the following March, his disgust at the number of saloon shootings was great: "Oriental [Saloon] a regular slaughterhouse now."

At several spots in his choppy narrative, Parsons jumps from the macabre to the everyday with a matter-of-fact rapidity that can sound unintentionally humorous.

After Luke Short shot Charley Storms outside the Oriental, Dr. Goodfellow brought to Parsons' room the bullet he removed from Storms' heart.

Parsons wrote: "Also showed a bloody handkerchief, part of which was carried into wound by pistol [sic, bullet]. Short, very unconcerned after shooting — probably a case of kill or be killed. Played Abbotts some chess tonight."

Most remarkable is the number of major events in which Parsons had a role: He was the first person confirmed a Christian at St. Paul's Episcopal Church, which still functions today; he was one of the few Tombstoners injured in the fire that swept the camp in June, 1880 (a porch collapsed on him as he helped fight the blaze); and he helped John P. Clum win election as mayor in January, 1881.

But Parsons' most recognized contribution was the record he left of the Earp-Clanton feud that has come to define Tombstone. He saw and commented on the unfolding drama, beginning with the October 28, 1880, shooting death of Marshal Fred White by bad man Curly Bill Brocius: "The Marshal was shot last night by one of the Texas cowboys and will probably die. . . . Will be a bad winter I'm afraid."

Matters were made worse by the cozy relationship between the cowboy gang and the sheriff's office, which Parsons decried: "Some of our officials should be hanged. They're a bad lot."

A year before the O.K. Corral fight, the town was struck by blinding lightning flashes and torrential rains. The lightning killed a man at Blinn's lumberyard, and Parsons wrote: "Of course — it is said — there must be a huge mineral deposit in immediate vicinity. A good vein is all that's wanted. Human life is secondary consideration altogether."

Parsons was out inspecting a mine the day of the fight, October 26, 1881. But he returned on October 27 to observe: "A bad time yesterday when Wyatt, Virgil and Morgan Earp with Doc Holliday had a street fight with the two McLowerys [McLaurys] and Bill Clanton and Ike, all but the latter being killed and V and M Earp wounded. Desperate men and a desperate encounter."

Two months later, he lamented the awful state of affairs: "I wish whiskey was all poured in gutter."

On the day of that entry, December 28, 1881, the cowboys ambushed Virgil Earp as he crossed Fifth Street. Parsons heard the four shotgun blasts "making a terrible noise."

Virgil, hit in the arm and back, was taken to a room at the Cosmopolitan Hotel. Parsons brought medicine and the next day wrote: "Elbow joint had to be taken out today and we've got that and some of the shattered bone in room. Patient doing well. It is surmised that Ike Clanton, Curly Bill and [William R] McLaury did the shooting."

After the O.K. Corral, the cowboys made various attempts to bring the Earps and Doc Holliday up on murder charges. One such effort, initiated by Ike Clanton, took place in mid-February, 1882: "Yesterday Earps were taken to Contention to be tried for the killing of Clanton. Quite a posse went out. Many of Earps' friends accompanied armed to the teeth. . . . Earps on one side of street with their friends and Ike Clanton and Ringo with theirs on the other side — watching each other. Blood will surely come."

Parsons was right. The following month, Morgan Earp

was fatally shot in the back. Parsons named Frank Stilwell as the probable killer and again demonstrated his macabre sense of timing: "For two cowardly, sneaking attempts at murder, this and the shots at Virgil E . . . rank at the head. Morg lived about 40 minutes and died without a murmur. . . . Attended church this morning. Bad time of it with boil."

Morgan's killing brought more bloodshed when Wyatt Earp rode off to seek revenge in what historians have come to call the Vendetta. Parsons was a member of the Committee of 100, an anti-cowboy vigilance committee, which perhaps explains his delight at Wyatt's subsequent killings.

On March 20, 1882, he wrote: "Tonight came news of Frank Stilwell's body being found riddled with bullets and buckshot. A quick vengeance and a bad character sent to hell, where he will be chief attraction until a few more accompany him."

Two days later, Wyatt caught up with Florentino Cruz, another of Morgan's murderers: "More killing by the Earp party. Hope they'll keep it up."

Wyatt made another hit, this one on Curly Bill at Iron Springs. Parsons noted it with glee on March 25: "I am heartily glad at this repulse and hope the killing is not stopped with the cut-throat named. Feeling is growing here against the ring, Sheriff [Johnny Behan], etc, and it would not surprise me to know of a necktie party some fine morning."

With the discovery of cowboy leader Johnny Ringo's body on Turkey Creek in July, 1882, the killing stopped. Parsons stayed five more years in Tombstone. When the mines played out, he left for Los Angeles.

"It was some time," he noted, "before I became accustomed to the freedom from the necessity of guarding our horses at night from rustlers and Apaches."

Parsons went on to become a respected businessman. He was a charter member and three-time director of the Los Angeles Chamber of Commerce. He kept his diary for almost 50 years, but no subject that drew his notice would ever be more compelling than the Earps of Tombstone.

He returned to the old camp in 1929, at age 79, and was feted as a special guest in the town's Helldorado celebration. But it wasn't George W. Parsons that everyone wanted to know about. It was Wyatt, Doc, and the cowboys.

Even on his return to California in January, 1887, one of the first people he met there was an Earp. His entry for January 15 reads: "Met Virgil Earp who looks well and seems to be doing well. Can use his arm some."

CHAPTER FIVE

THE BROTHERS EARP

Romanticized and vilified, this one family
struggled for a dream out West
that was not to be. Instead of success built
on their hard work, the Earps found
pain, death, and notoriety.

BY BOB BOZE BELL

WHEN WYATT EARP, HIS BROTHERS, AND THEIR FAMILIES arrived in Tombstone in late November, 1879, every available house was taken. So the Earps rented a one-bedroom adobe on Allen Street. No floor, just hard-packed dirt. The price? $40 a month. The Earps rolled up their sleeves, fixed the roof, drove the wagons up on each side and took the wagon sheets off the bows to stretch out for more room. They cooked in the fireplace and used boxes for chairs.

The Earp women took jobs sewing complete tents and canvas awnings for the new stores and shops going up right and left. The Earp men got jobs bartending and doing odd jobs in the gambling halls. Wyatt also got a job as shotgun messenger (a job he later passed on to his brother, Morgan).

Wyatt initially intended to start a stage line in Tombstone, but he was dissuaded when he arrived to find two companies already in stiff competition (a price war had cut passenger rates to $4 for the trip from Benson to Tombstone).

Later, when they got a foothold, the Earp families set up three households on the west end of town at First and Fremont streets, which was not considered a "good" area of town by the upper crust.

Years later, Virgil's wife Allie, remembered: "We weren't

rich minin' folks and important business people, and we lived across the Dead Line."

As one of the social matrons of Tombstone put it, "The line was pretty well-drawn those days. Ordinary women didn't mix with the wives of gamblers, no matter what pretty dresses they had or how nice they were. And the Misses Earp were all good, but they were in that fix and we just naturally didn't have much to do with them."

The snobbery was not confined to women.

"How men of good family and connections East can come here and marry prostitutes — take them out of a dance house — I can't see," wrote George Parsons in his Tombstone journal. Although Parsons wasn't naming names, he might well have been referring to the Earps.

Wyatt had met his live-in companion, Mattie Blaylock, in a Kansas dance house (Wyatt's first wife died in 1870 during childbirth). His younger brother, Morgan, also had met his live-in companion, Louisa, in a similar place.

Wyatt came to Tombstone with Mattie, and they lived together as man and wife, although there is no record of their marriage. In fact, of the four Earp couples, only Jim and Bessie enjoyed the formality of a wedding ceremony.

The Earp brothers and their common-law wives lived on the margins of Tombstone society (Virgil was declined admittance into the local Masonic Lodge). Regardless of their social standing, the Earps intended to stake a claim on the American dream, pooling their resources to make a financial difference in the quality of their lives.

Within a year, they began to see results. In fact, after all their Western wanderings, it looked like the Earps had finally found the bonanza they were seeking. Wyatt and his brothers owned all, or part of, 10 mines. In August of 1880, the brothers sold a set of lots for $6,000, and then in November, Wyatt and a partner sold the Comstock mine for $3,000. The Earp combine was flush with cash and ready to invest even more, but the events of October, 1881, destroyed everything.

WYATT EARP

The "cowboy crowd" ranged from San Simon to the Mexican border. They were part of a loose-knit fraternity of "stockmen" who weren't afraid to use physical force to protect their territory against outsiders — which, to them, included Indians, Mexicans, the federal government, and the Earps.

A hotel operator in Galeyville said of the cowboys: "They do not work, and they are never without money. . . . They are not all brave, and often sneak away from danger, but . . . I never knew one of them to whine and squeal when he knew he had to die. They will run away from death, but when cornered will look into the muzzle of a six-shooter with defiant indifference."

He could well have been describing the Clantons and McLaurys, ranching families connected by rural interests and

MORGAN EARP

self-preservation. Even though both families engaged in shady cattle deals, to this day there are more than a few who believe their only sin was to be in the wrong place at the wrong time.

While in Tombstone, a young dancer from San Francisco named Josephine "Sadie" Marcus lived openly as Mrs. Johnny Behan, even though she and Cochise County Sheriff Behan were not married. (In later years she insisted on being called Josie, but everyone in Tombstone knew her as Sadie.) Miss Marcus was Behan's prized possession, and Behan was Wyatt Earp's most adamant rival.

At some point, "Mrs. Behan," as 19-year-old Sadie signed herself around town, became disenchanted with the sheriff (Behan was a notorious womanizer) and took up with the deputy U.S. marshal — Wyatt Earp. When and how this relationship began is lost to history, but between December of

1880 and March of 1882, a romance was born that drove another wedge between the two lawmen and ultimately ruined Wyatt's "marriage" to Mattie.

A flurry of stagecoach robberies plagued Cochise County in early 1881, capped off by the March 15 Benson stage robbery in which a driver and passenger were killed.

Wyatt said he wanted the "glory" of capturing the perpetrators of the Benson stage robbery so he could be elected sheriff in the next election, dethroning Behan. Earp made a deal with the leader of the rustlers, Ike Clanton, and others, to give up the Benson stage robbers — Leonard, Crane, and Head — in exchange for the Wells Fargo reward. The deal went south when the stage robbers were killed by others in New Mexico. To make matters worse, Clanton believed that Wyatt leaked his traitorous intentions about the "deal" to Doc Holliday. Consequently, Clanton made threats against the Earps in order to cover his tracks and distance himself from the appearance of fraternizing with the enemy.

On the evening of October 25, while taking in the town with cowboy friend Tom McLaury, Ike Clanton "bucked the tiger" (played faro) and cruised Allen Street, careful not to miss any bars. At around 11 P.M., he stepped into the Alhambra lunch counter for a bite.

While there, he was confronted by Doc Holliday, who raked him over the coals for his cowardice and his accusations. Although Clanton tried to act tough, Holliday thoroughly humiliated him until Morgan Earp pulled the dentist outside. But Clanton followed Holliday, and more words were exchanged before Virgil arrived and threatened to arrest them both if they didn't stop. Drunk and full of false courage, Clanton later confronted Wyatt outside the Eagle Brewery and told him that in the morning he would have "man for man."

Believing Clanton to be all hot air, Wyatt, Morgan, and Holliday went to their separate homes and retired for the night.

Meanwhile, Clanton was just hitting his stride as he played in an all-night poker game in the Occidental Saloon. Among the players: Tom McLaury, Virgil Earp, and Johnny Behan.

By morning, Clanton was full of whiskey and more threats. He told anyone who would listen, "Fight is my racket. All I want is four feet of ground." Much to Clanton's later distress, his request would soon be granted.

By 2 P.M., five cowboys congregated in a vacant lot between two buildings on west Fremont — Ike Clanton (totally soused), Bill Clanton, Tom McLaury, Frank McLaury, and Billy Claiborne. A cold wind whipped around the corners of the frame house as they stamped their feet and tried to keep warm. They cursed the cold and the Earps while passing a bottle among themselves. Snow flurries were later reported in the mountains.

Sheriff Behan came down and tried to disarm the cowboys. They refused, saying they would only lay off their arms if the Earps did also, and besides, they, the cowboys, were leaving town.

Starting from Hafford's Corner, Virgil, Wyatt, Morgan, and Doc Holliday started walking up Fourth towards Fremont. Their mission, according to City Marshal Virgil Earp, was to disarm the cowboys.

However, Wyatt said a telling thing to Doc before they left. He said, "This isn't your fight." Those are more the words of a gunman looking for a fight than the words of a lawman.

Holliday replied, "That's a hell of a thing for you to say to me." Also not the words of a peacekeeper.

Virgil had given Holliday the Wells Fargo shotgun and told him to discreetly put it under his coat. Meanwhile, Virgil carried Doc's cane and led the foursome past the post office, then west onto Fremont.

Sheriff Behan, still talking to the cowboys, saw the approaching Earps, came up the street, and tried to stop them, but he was unsuccessful. The Earps and Holliday kept on walking past him to confront the cowboys in the narrow lot (15 to 18 feet, according to witnesses) between Fly's boardinghouse and the Harwood house.

VIRGIL EARP

Four cowboys remained to face the Earps and Holliday: Ike Clanton with his 19-year-old brother, Billy, and Tom and Frank McLaury. Billy Claiborne had faded from the field.

Virgil immediately tried to arrest the cowboys by telling them to give up their guns, but something alarmed Billy Clanton and Frank McLaury (probably the menacing shotgun that Holliday suddenly brandished). There was a "click-click" as the two cowboys cocked their weapons, followed by two shots reverberating almost as one.

Wyatt claimed the first two shots were fired by him and Billy Clanton. It was later estimated that 30 shots were fired in 27 seconds. When it was over, three of the cowboys were dead and two of the Earps wounded.

A hearing was held to decide if there was enough evidence for a murder charge. Wyatt and Doc spent time in jail (Morgan and Virgil were dismissed because of their wounds).

The Earps were ultimately exonerated and tried to carry on their lives in Tombstone, but the trouble had only begun.

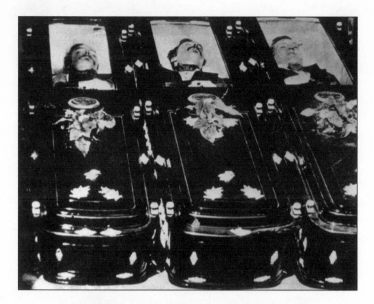

**SHOWN IN THEIR COFFINS (LEFT TO RIGHT),
TOM MCLAURY, FRANK MCLAURY, AND BILLY CLANTON,
WHO DIED IN THE SHOOT-OUT NEAR THE O.K. CORRAL.**

On December 28, 1881, Virgil Earp was shot from an ambush. He miraculously survived, although he would remain a cripple for life. Three months later, Morgan Earp was murdered — shot in the back — while he played pool in Hatch's Saloon. Wyatt went on a vendetta ride with Doc and others, killing several of those whom he suspected of being in on his brother's killing.

Now wanted for murder, Wyatt and Doc Holliday fled to Colorado via New Mexico.

Wyatt and his brothers had only been in Tombstone for 22 months. But no matter where he went or what he did after that, the ghosts of Tombstone were never far behind.

Abandoned by Wyatt, Mattie returned to "the line" (prostitution) and died of a laudanum overdose in 1888.

Wyatt and his surviving brothers ping-ponged across the

West, operating saloons in San Diego, Cripple Creek, Seattle, and numerous other western boomtowns.

Wyatt and Sadie joined the gold rush to Alaska in 1897. Wyatt refereed prize fights (he holds the dubious distinction of being the only referee in California boxing history to be disarmed before a fight could begin) and prospected around the Colorado River area near Parker, Arizona. He continued to prospect and gamble well into his 70s. He also befriended movie people in Hollywood and acted as a movie consultant for William S. Hart and Tom Mix.

Warren Earp was shot dead in a drinking quarrel in 1900. Virgil died of pneumonia in Goldfield, Nevada, in 1905. Allie Earp died in 1945. Wyatt's third wife, Sadie, died in 1944.

Until his dying day, Wyatt Earp could never appreciate the public's fascination with the tragic events of Tombstone. To him and the rest of the Earp family, it was a horrific memory of personal loss and failed dreams.

Beginning with the 1929 celebration of Tombstone's first Helldorado Days, many of the old Tombstoners who attended were as bewildered as Wyatt to see the Earp-Clanton feud as the focal point of their legacy.

John Clum, in particular, was very upset.

He wrote: "The mock street battle between the city police and the rustlers was a grim exhibition that should have been omitted. The spectacle of men engaged in mortal combat is repulsive and distressing. It is inconceivable that any normal spectator derived either pleasure or benefit from viewing the mock battle. The lamentable clash between the city police and the rustlers on October 26, 1881, occasioned more partisan bitterness than anything else that ever occurred in the community — and traces of that bitterness linger to this day. There was no justification for the inclusion of that gruesome act in the Helldorado program, and in my judgment, the mock street fight was reprehensible."

With the subsequent deluge of books, movies, and television shows, followed by the 1993-94 release of two major motion pictures about Wyatt and the events of Tombstone, the "town too tough to die" has seen a resurgence of tourists flocking in from all over the world. Tens of thousands visit each year to "see where they walked" and "see where they fell."

The so-called Gunfight at the O.K. Corral is reenacted almost daily, with multiple reenactments on the weekends and holidays. The mock street fight has become the very engine of the local economy: a cash cow, the centerpiece, the defining moment of Tombstone's long history. Think about it: 30 seconds out of 100-plus years.

The stone-cold irony was not lost on one avid aficionado who had just witnessed his umpteenth reenactment of the shoot-out.

"History is indeed a cruel trick played on the dead by the living," he said with a sad smile.

BIG NOSE KATE

*She lived a wild and woolly life
on her own terms — and under several different
names. More than just "Doc Holliday's woman,"
Kate was perhaps the toughest of them all.*

B Y   L E O   W.   B A N K S

<hr>

MARY KATHARINE HARONY HATED WYATT EARP BUT
loved Doc Holliday. She roamed the West with both
men, and her name is part of the Earp legend — at
least one of her names is. But in later years, she wanted no
one to know that she was born to European aristocracy and
spoke several languages. Or that she had been involved in a few
shooting scrapes and once torched a Texas town to save Doc's
hide. But most of all, Mary Katharine did not want it known that
she'd once been a frontier madam known as Big Nose Kate.

That unforgettable nickname is well known to followers
of the Tombstone story, but Kate's extraordinary life is not.
The most important information about her came to light through
sheer chance.

In 1976, an Iowa newspaper columnist reported on writer
Glenn Boyer's search for Kate's family. In response, an Illinois
woman wrote to say she had something that might interest
Boyer.

What she had was Kate's autobiography, brief but rich
in never-revealed recollections. The document had been found
stuffed into a book once owned by Kate's late niece, Lillie
Raffert. Ironically, the book was a copy of *Wyatt Earp: Frontier
Marshal*, Stuart Lake's 1931 biography of Earp.

Kate called Lake's work "a bunch of lies," and with reason. Lake identified her as Kate Fisher, not her true name;

BIG NOSE KATE, BORN MARY KATHARINE HARONY,
WAS SOMETIMES KNOWN AS KATE ELDER.

published a photo purporting to be her but wasn't; and dismissed her as a dance-hall girl, which was only half true.

There was more to her, but maybe Lake didn't find out because of the way Kate lived — taking and shedding names like clothing, trying out one frontier town after another, always running from some past indelicacy, or worse.

She was born in Budapest, Hungary, on November 7, 1850. In the early 1860s, her physician father, Michael Harony, along with other well-off European families, accompanied Maximilian to Mexico City. French troops had conquered Mexico, and Maximilian was named the country's emperor. The Haronys eventually left Mexico for Davenport, Iowa, where Kate's father and mother, Katharina Boldizar, died within months of each other in 1865.

Placed in a guardian's care, Kate ran away and wound up a stowaway on a Mississippi River steamboat. The captain took a liking to the strong-willed teenager and arranged for her to live at a St. Louis convent.

She called herself Kate Elder but would later change that to Fisher, and for a time, she was also Kate Melvin, from a brief marriage to Silas Melvin. By 1874, Kate worked in a Wichita brothel controlled by Bessie Earp, wife of Wyatt's brother, Jim. While there, Kate was fined for prostitution.

Also in Kansas, according to Boyer, Kate fell in love with Wyatt Earp. Boyer believes that Earp broke off the affair, creating an enmity that intensified when Kate fell for Doc and found herself trapped between the two men.

She often complained about the eerie hold Earp had over Holliday, how the tubercular dentist seemed willing to follow Earp wherever he went. "He (Doc) was always kind to me until he got mixed up with the Earps," Kate told pioneer and writer Anton Mazzanovich. "That changed everything between Doc and me."

Where Kate and Holliday met is uncertain. It's also unclear what Holliday thought of how she earned her money. But author Jane Candia Coleman, in a novel about Kate's life titled *Doc Holliday's Woman*, depicts the tempestuous Kate exploding in rage at Doc's questions about Wichita:

"How do you think I managed? Nobody respectable would give me a job. If Bessie hadn't, I'd have died on the street, and if you don't like it, you can go to hell."

Fiction, perhaps, but given the facts of frontier life and Kate's personality, Coleman's words sound plausible.

Kate was with Holliday in Fort Griffin, Texas, in 1877, when gambler Ed Bailey trifled with Holliday at the poker tables. It was Bailey with a six-shooter versus Holliday with a knife. No contest. Doc eviscerated Bailey.

He was arrested and in danger of hanging, but Kate set fire to the hotel where Doc was being held and jammed a pistol into the belly of his guard. The two rode several hundred miles on stolen horses, the law choking on their dust.

The list of towns in which they dallied grew — Deadwood in the Dakotas, as well as Trinidad, Colorado, and Las Vegas, New Mexico, where they stayed about two years.

Once, the authorities came to arrest Doc. Believing they were going to kill him, Kate marched onto the front porch in her nightgown and stood them off with a pistol. "If you want anything, come and get it," she said.

She also found Doc with another woman. "I had a big knife with me and said I'd rip her open," Kate said. That separated the two, probably for good.

They weren't a popular couple in Las Vegas, judging by descriptions published in the *Optic* newspaper. It called Doc "a "shiftless, bagged-legged character — a killer and a professional cut-throat and not a whit too refined to rob stages or even steal sheep." And Kate was "a Santa Fe tid bit who surrounded her habiliments with a detestable odor before leaving the Ancient City that will, in itself, make her memory immortal."

In the fall of 1879, at Wyatt's request, Doc and Kate began making their way to Tombstone, but Kate refused to live there. She headed for the mining town of Globe instead, using $500 to buy a hotel, which probably served the local miners much more than supper.

"I wanted Doc to go with me," Kate wrote in her memoir, dated March 18, 1940, to her niece. "The Earps had such power I could not get Doc away from them."

The Earps were one of many subjects that brought her and Holliday to screaming fits. Their nastiest battle came in 1881, after the Benson stagecoach holdup, which left two men dead, on March 15.

Kate, full of whiskey and angry with Doc after another blowup, signed a statement saying Holliday committed the robbery. She was urged on by Sheriff Johnny Behan, who then arrested Holliday, but the charge was dropped when Kate recanted.

Lake wrote that shortly after leaving court, Holliday handed Kate $1,000 as an inducement to disappear.

"That evening," Lake wrote, "Big-Nosed Kate left Tombstone, and as far as Wyatt Earp ever knew, she and Doc Holliday parted company forever."

But they didn't part forever, at least not according to

**JOHN "DOC" HOLLIDAY, CIRCA 1882,
IN A PHOTOGRAPH CREDITED TO C.S. FLY.**

Kate's own account. She was back in Tombstone on October 26, 1881, the day of the O.K. Corral gunfight, staying with Doc at Fly's boardinghouse.

Awaking before Doc that morning, she spotted a man in the hall. His head was bandaged, and he carried a rifle. She later learned from Mollie Fly that it was an angry Ike Clanton, asking Doc's whereabouts.

"I told Doc Ike Clanton was looking for him," Kate wrote. "Doc said, 'If God will let me live to get my clothes on, he shall see me.'

"With that he got up, dressed and went out. As he went out he said, 'I may not be back to take you to breakfast, so you better go alone.' I didn't go to breakfast. I don't remember of eating anything that day."

But she remembered the shooting. In her memoir, spelling errors and all, she described it as she saw it through Mollie Fly's window:

"I saw four men coming from the livery stable on Allen Street coming to the vacant lot. Almost at the same time I saw Virgil Earp, Wyet, Morgan Earp and Doc Holliday coming to the vacant lot from Fremont Street. They stood ten feet apart when the shooting began.

"Ike Clanton run and left his young brother, Billy. I saw Doc fall, but he was up as quick as he fell. Something went wrong with his rifle, he threw his rifle on the ground & pulled out his six shooter. Every shot he fired got a man. . . . It is foolish to think that a cow rusuller gun man can come up to a city gun man in a gun fight."

Historians believe that last remark refers to the fact that since cowboys couldn't afford extra shells, they couldn't target practice.

Kate was still running her Globe hotel in 1887 when Doc's health failed. He was in a Glenwood Springs, Colorado, sanitorium, and she rushed there to say good-bye.

Her love for Doc never waned, but neither did her hatred for Wyatt. She sullied his name at every opportunity, even alleging he was a stage robber in his Tombstone days. She told Mazzanovich and others a patently false tale about Wyatt's penchant for packing disguises, such as false mustaches, beards, and wigs, which he used to pull off his alleged holdups.

After finally leaving behind Holliday and Earp, Kate moved often and took at least one more name. In 1888, she married blacksmith George Cummings. They lived in Bisbee and Pearce until she divorced him because of his drinking in 1898.

At the turn of the century, she worked as a maid at the Cochise Hotel, then as a housekeeper to John J. Howard, a solid miner and farmer from Dos Cabezas with whom she remained until his death in 1930.

Kate's last stop was the Arizona Pioneers' Home in Prescott. It had a policy against admitting foreigners, so Kate lied about her birthplace and got in. She found a good life there, clipping bond coupons and braiding rugs. Very few knew who she was and what she'd done. Kate wanted it that way, although, as she wrote in her memoir, a little cash might coax from her a story or two.

"There are quite a few that want me to write up things, but as they don't want to give me anything I don't write."

Kate broke her no-interview rule when she met with friend A.W. Bork in 1935. Her intention was to sell her story to one of the big magazines, as Lake had done. The memoir produced from that meeting, coupled with Kate's letter to Raffert, provides much of what is now known about her.

But no one was interested in buying Kate's story. Bork found her pleasant company anyway, saying: "She was a trim, well-spoken little old lady and, like a lot of them then, seeking respectability in old age. For example, she always claimed she and Doc Holliday were married."

That claim of marriage was probably false, another sidestep in a life that can only be described as a cunning triumph. As Coleman says, she did what was necessary to survive, and on the frontier, that was the only avocation required for a woman who didn't teach or take in laundry.

Mary Katharine Harony died November 2, 1940, at 89. She rests on the grounds of the Pioneers' Home under a marker that reads Mary K. Cummings.

CHAPTER SEVEN

JOHN BEHAN

Once Wyatt Earp's biggest rival in Tombstone,
John Behan lost a bright future,
ending his days in obscurity.
Was he really a villain in the Tombstone saga — or
just the man who came in second best to Wyatt?

BY LEO W. BANKS

—————

JOHNNY BEHAN, COCHISE COUNTY'S FIRST SHERIFF, CAME within a whisker of winning history's admiration. Author J.H. McClintock, writing four years after Behan's death in 1912, described him as a man who won "the respect and esteem of all with whom he came in contact" and lived a life "varied in service and faultless in honor."

But Behan's memory lost that respect and esteem with the 1931 publication of *Wyatt Earp, Frontier Marshal*. Stuart Lake's biography turned a lasting spotlight on Wyatt Earp that showed up the character of the men around him. That bright light didn't flatter Johnny Behan.

He was a slick politician with too many friends, a balding playboy who enjoyed a good romp with a prostitute, loved money, and was downright intimate with whiskey. Tombstone diarist George Parsons called him "our rascally sheriff."

Still, he served in numerous public positions and often served well. Before coming to Tombstone, John Harris Behan seemed intent on filling every public chair that would hold him. Most of those positions were in Prescott, then the Territorial capital, where he started as a clerk in the first Territorial Legislature. In 1866, at age 20, he was appointed Yavapai County deputy sheriff, his first lawman's job.

Following that, he was undersheriff, county recorder, county clerk, and in 1871, he won election as Yavapai's sheriff. He also served in the Seventh and Tenth Legislative Assemblies, making the political contacts to which he would turn throughout his life.

Even as he lived as a public man, Behan always fixed one eye on his own interests. His reason for originally coming West in 1863 — from Westport, Missouri, where he was born in 1845 — testifies to that.

"My mother's sentiments in the war were southern and my father's union," he once explained. "But in any event, I wasn't interested in stopping a mini-ball for either side."

While the *Arizona Miner* newspaper called Behan one of the best sheriffs Yavapai County had ever had, those Prescott years also laid bare his character's weaknesses.

In 1869, he married Victoria Zaff in San Francisco. Six years later, she filed for divorce in Prescott. Victoria Behan's 1875 divorce complaint, on file at the Arizona Historical Society, detailed his carnal adventures with a prostitute named Sada Mansfield. These wrongs were "committed openly and notoriously, causing great scandal in Prescott."

Behan was ordered to pay $16.66 a month in support of their son, Albert, then four.

Before leaving Prescott, Behan had a violent encounter with angry Chinese citizens. The *Miner*, in an account lacking detail but certainly not bias, wrote on October 3, 1879:

"Hon. John H. Behan had occasion to call at the Chinese laundry this P.M., when a controversy arose, leading to some half-dozen of the pig-tail race making an assault on him with clubs. He tried to defend himself with a revolver, which, unfortunately, failed to work. He received several cuts about the head."

A week later, he left Prescott to become a deputy sheriff in Gillette (also Gillett), a mining camp north of Phoenix.

Two months after taking the job in Gillette, Behan was riding in a posse pursuing Mexican highwaymen when he met

Josephine Sarah Marcus. The 18-year-old actress was traveling by stagecoach with a theater troupe.

Judging by Behan's reaction to her, Josephine possessed a manner and build sufficient to make a man strap his chaps on backward. Or at least make rash promises. To Josephine, he pledged marriage, and the two eventually made their way to Tombstone.

Behan lived with Josie nearly a year. When she realized he wasn't going to make good on his vow, the relationship ended. Josie took up with Wyatt Earp, sowing the seeds for future hostility.

The two men's enmity intensified when Behan reneged on another promise. Cochise County was formed February 1, 1881, with Tombstone made its county seat. (The county seat was later moved to Bisbee.) Behan won appointment as the new county's first sheriff. He had promised to name Wyatt Earp as his deputy but never did.

Behan's county badge didn't change his womanizing, except to make it worse. Pioneer Charles Liftchild recalled that the sheriff constantly competed with businessman Jim Vizina "to capture the good graces of every actress and prominent beauty arriving, regardless of cost of champagne and gifts."

The two regularly appeared in the gallery boxes at the Bird Cage Theatre, where they were well placed to assess the passing talent.

"On such occasions," Liftchild wrote in his memoirs, "betting would result among many as to which would later capture the affections of the reigning beauty. Vizina would generally win."

So it was in Behan's dealings with Earp, too. He was always second best.

On March 15, 1881, cowboys held up a stagecoach near Benson and murdered two men. A posse, which included both Earp and Sheriff Behan, arrested Luther King and deposited him in jail.

But King didn't stay there long. The last thing Behan

JOHN BEHAN, CIRCA 1883.

wanted was for his rival to get the credit for exposing and breaking up the bandit ring, so he arranged for King's "escape." Behan also tried to discredit Earp by hanging the Benson murders on his notorious friend, Doc Holliday.

It was a transparent effort by a sheriff whose sympathies were never hard to trace. Behan was a Southerner and a Democrat, in league with the cowboy-rustler gang whose criminal enterprises were being thwarted by the Republican Earps.

With the O.K. Corral incident later that year, Sheriff Behan was ineffectual, corrupt, or both. He met the Earp party as it walked purposefully toward the showdown and told Wyatt he'd disarmed the cowboys waiting near the corral.

In truth, the cowboys had refused the sheriff's order to turn over their weapons. It can never be proved, but Behan might well have hoped the misinformation would cause the Earps to drop their guard.

When the shooting stopped, and wagons were brought in to retrieve the bodies, Behan tried to arrest Wyatt.

"You have deceived me, Johnny," Earp responded. "You told me they were not armed. I won't be arrested, but I am here to answer for what I have done. I am not going to leave town."

It wouldn't be the only time Behan tried to arrest Wyatt Earp. The second time, March 21, 1882, Behan had in his pocket a warrant for Earp's arrest for killing Frank Stilwell the day before at the Tucson train yard. (Stilwell, a former Behan deputy, was thought by many — particularly Wyatt Earp — to be the triggerman in Morgan Earp's ambush murder.)

When Behan told Earp he'd like to see him, Earp responded, "Johnny, you may see me once too often." Behan backed off again.

He later mounted a posse, consisting of such sterling citizens as gunman Johnny Ringo, to chase the Earp party as it left Arizona Territory. Stuart Lake wrote that Behan even went to Fort Grant to try to enlist the aid of Apache scouts in the hunt.

But many writers later said he never wanted to catch Earp at all. At the time, Tombstoner George Parsons noted in his diary: "He [Behan] organizes posses, goes to within a mile of his prey and then returns. He's a good one."

Some believe Behan's corruption even extended to paying to have Morgan Earp assassinated. Holliday certainly thought so. He went around Tombstone kicking in doors, looking for the men he believed were behind Morgan's murder. One of them was Behan.

Still, some who knew Behan in Tombstone admired him.

In his book, *Brewery Gulch: Frontier Days of Old Arizona,* old-timer Joe Chisholm told of an incident after the O.K. Corral. Two of the Earps and Holliday strolled into the Oriental Saloon and were met by owner Milt Joyce, who obviously believed Behan's ruse about the Benson stage holdup.

"Look who's here," Joyce sniffed. "I suppose there will be another stage holdup by morning."

One of the Earps, probably Wyatt, slapped Joyce across the face, and the other Earp and Holliday drew their guns. The incident ended there.

But the next day, Wyatt, Virgil, and Holliday were playing faro in the rear of another saloon when a still-angry Joyce stormed in, a sidearm in each fist.

"Do you sons of bitches want a fight as badly as you did last night?" he demanded.

No one in the Earp party moved.

"Behan had seen Joyce headed for the saloon and knew he was heeled," Chisholm wrote. "The sheriff got in the place just as Joyce had bluffed the three of them cold. . . . He [Behan] seized Joyce from behind, pinioned his arms, turned his back squarely upon his enemies . . . and carried Joyce outside and placed him under arrest."

Another account had Behan explaining his actions by saying, "There's been enough killing in Tucson."

Overall, though, Behan's Tombstone career did not cover him with glory. He lost the sheriff's election in November, 1882, and a grand jury indicted him for continuing to collect taxes after his term expired.

The district attorney, another political friend, made the charge go away. But disappearing funds and suspicions about his handling of public money was a recurring theme in Behan's career.

After Tombstone, Behan led an unspectacular life in various public offices. He was assistant superintendent and later superintendent of the Yuma Territorial Prison; customs inspector at Buffalo, New Orleans, and El Paso; a Chinese

Exclusion Inspector along the Mexican border; and the business manager of the *Tucson Citizen* newspaper.

He served in Cuba as an attaché of the quartermaster's department during the Spanish-American war, and he went with the U.S. Army to China during the Boxer Rebellion.

During these years, he was dogged by minor troubles, such as drinking too much and earning a reprimand for doctoring his government expense accounts.

In Yuma in 1890, a drunken Behan tried to drive his horse-drawn buggy into a hotel lobby. When he was stopped, he got angry and shot the place up. Headline writers called the embarrassment "Johnny's Jamboree."

Only 49, Behan died of Bright's disease at St. Mary's Hospital in Tucson. His burial site remained a mystery until 1990, when Tombstone author Ben Traywick discovered his unmarked grave at the city's Holy Hope Cemetery.

Traywick and some other Tombstoners didn't think it was right that a famous, if flawed, pioneer should rest in a plot without a marker. They chipped in to buy him one. "He'd probably be very happy to find out that somebody else paid for it," Traywick said.

CHAPTER EIGHT

C.S. & MOLLIE FLY

*Without their photographs to show us, many
eloquent faces of the Old West
would be lost and forgotten.
But this plucky pair of frontier photographers
paid a high price to live on history's doorstep.*

BY PETER ALESHIRE

<hr>

B RILLIANT PHOTOGRAPHER, MEDIOCRE SHERIFF, AND failed miner — Camillus Sidney Fly lived a life of great risks, frustrated dreams, and blunted hopes, but his photographs captured some of the most famous images in the history of the west.

The Tombstone photographer used his bulky camera to make glass-slide images of some of the defining moments of Western history — including negotiations between Geronimo's band of about 32 Apache renegades and Gen. George Crook. A century later, these hardened warriors still gaze into the un-blinking camera lens with a terrible and somber dignity, as though they knew this would become a final record of a doomed way of life.

Fly produced 5,000 images of the Apache campaigns which raged across the Sonoran desert until Geronimo's final surrender in 1886. They constitute his most enduring legacy in an eventful career that included witnessing the gunfight at the O.K. Corral, photographing some of the most famous heroes and villains in the Southwest, searching for silver, chasing out-laws as sheriff of Cochise County, and chronicling earthquakes and fires.

Fly's mother inexplicably named him Camillus Sidney, after a Roman general. It proved an unfortunate name for a

Missouri boy born in 1849. So he went first by his initials and later by the nickname "Buck," for the buckboard in which he carried his photographic equipment.

In 1879, Fly met and married Mary (Mollie) Edith Goodrich, age 30, in California. Mollie was already working as a photographer in San Francisco. One friend later said of Mollie, "She was 5 feet of pure dignity and beauty, always plainly dressed and with the bearing and manner of a queen."

An accomplished photographer in her own right and an adventurous woman, Mollie Fly followed her husband from one exciting, failed dream to another. Initially, the couple operated a photography studio in San Francisco, the cosmopolitan hub of the West. But the business faltered, and news of a silver strike in Tombstone hit the San Francisco papers.

Fly made a hasty trip to the rapidly growing mining town, in the midst of territory still plagued by gunfights, thieves, and warfare with the Apaches. Infected by the possibilities, he hurried home, sold his business, and moved his new wife to a town still composed mostly of tents and shanties. Within a few years, rich veins of silver had transformed Tombstone into the biggest city between St. Louis and San Francisco.

Camillus brimmed with plans and relied heavily on Mollie's business sense, skill as a photographer, and moral support to see them accomplished. The Flys built a boardinghouse and an adjoining photographic studio at 312 Fremont Street, next to the O.K. Corral, and advertised "colored work and instantaneous photographs — copies may be had at any time."

Mollie ran the boardinghouse as well as the photographic studio. One of their first boarders was Doc Holiday's girlfriend "Big Nose Kate," a hard-drinking, hard-living woman who opened Tombstone's first whorehouse in a hastily erected tent.

Fly soon found himself busy taking formal portraits of the town's leading citizens, cowboys, and assorted characters. The residents of Tombstone seemed eager to stoke the developing mythology of the West, since they posed with the rifles, pistols, and props Fly supplied.

**ONE OF THE FEW PHOTOGRAPHS OF CAMILLUS S. FLY,
SHOWN HERE MOUNTED ON THE HORSE
IN FOREGROUND, CIRCA 1882.**

Occasionally, Fly stumbled into confrontations. When he offended one local woman, she promptly built a tall fence next to his studio, cutting off the sunlight and effectively putting him out of business. He quickly made amends, and she pulled the fence down.

But mostly he seemed to have avoided the factions that roiled Tombstone. He and Mollie had no children, but they did take in two young girls without homes, Cora Henry and Kitty Patterson.

Cora Henry later noted: "The Flys were good, kind people. I never heard them say an unkind word to anyone or do an unkind act." She described Fly as a tall, gentle man with a knack for convincing people to sit for pictures.

**MOLLIE FLY, CIRCA 1885,
PROBABLY TAKEN BY C.S. FLY.**

And he took some extraordinary pictures. He document-
ed the fires that periodically destroyed most of Tombstone, a
massive earthquake in Mexico, the life of a miner, local lynch-
ings, and mass executions. He journeyed often into the field
to take portraits of soldiers on payday, charging 35 cents each.

Curiously, Fly seemingly failed to photograph the most
famous event in Tombstone's tumultuous history, the gunfight
at the O.K. Corral. Fly's evident failure to document the gunfight
next door to his studio has intrigued historians.

It occurred on his doorstep, several participants fled
through his studio, and Fly himself removed the gun from Billy
Clanton's dying hand.

But Fly left no pictures of the gunfight or of the biggest

funeral in Tombstone history, in which the bodies of the Clanton gang were escorted to Boothill under a banner proclaiming "Murdered In The Streets of Tombstone." Nor did Fly leave any photographs relating to the later shooting of Virgil Earp or the assassination of Morgan Earp.

Why not?

Such questions still dog accounts of the infamous gunfight. Earp supporters maintain that the Earps killed Billy Clanton and Frank and Tom McLaury in self-defense when those longtime foes of the Earps went for their guns rather than surrender them in accordance with the law against carrying firearms in the town limits.

Critics of the Earps insist that the mostly unarmed Clanton group was leaving town when the Earps opened fire without warning. The conflict between the Earps and the Clanton "cowboy" faction had divided and embittered Tombstone politics for several years. After the gunfight and resulting assassinations, many of the law-abiding citizens turned on Earp and his supporters.

Did Fly avoid embroilment in these deep waters by simply not taking pictures of these famous events? Did he destroy photographs that might have damaged one side or the other? Did he avoid taking pictures to protect the Earps, with whom he generally sympathized?

Fortunately for posterity, Fly didn't miss out on the conclusion of Arizona Territory's Apache wars. He attached himself to General Crook's party when the general passed by Tombstone on his way to negotiate with Geronimo and his fellow Chiricahua Apaches.

Two decades of intermittent warfare had finally forced most of the Apaches to submit, but Geronimo, Naiche, Nana, and up to 110 followers bolted from the White Mountain Apache reservation in May, 1885, and cut a bloody swath across the Southwest. General Crook scoured the rugged landscape with one-quarter of the nation's standing army, but couldn't catch the handful of remaining warriors. But Crook had the time to wait.

Weary with the unending struggle, fearful of the inevitable end, and longing for the families and friends who had already been shipped to exile in Florida, the Apaches finally agreed to meet with Crook in Mexico at the Canon de los Embudos to discuss surrender terms. Crook found the Apaches encamped on a commanding hill about 500 yards from where the Indians told the soldiers to camp.

General Crook undertook three days of negotiations, promising the Apaches that if they surrendered, they wouldn't be punished for past crimes. Instead, he promised, they would be shipped to exile in Florida for two years before being allowed to return to a reservation in Arizona.

Fly produced 19 views of 17 different scenes during these negotiations. Only the first photograph in the series is truly spontaneous, a picture of Geronimo and other Apache leaders sitting beneath a cluster of cottonwoods and willows in one of their first conversations with Crook and his officers. Fly carefully composed the other pictures, directing the warriors to take up well-composed positions.

Capt. John G. Bourke described how Fly, with such "'nerve' that would have reflected undying glory on a Chicago drummer coolly asked 'Geronimo' and the warriors with him to change positions, and turn their heads or faces to improve the negative."

After the Apaches withdrew to debate Crook's terms, Fly and his assistant boldly walked into their encampment and asked them to pose for a series of photos, the only pictures ever taken of Apaches, under arms, in the field.

"He was a d——d fool for going into the camp," Bourke said. Fortunately, the Apaches proved cooperative.

However, Geronimo and 35 followers soon changed their minds about surrendering, partly as a result of the liquor and rumors supplied by an unscrupulous Army beef contractor. The contractor apparently stirred up trouble on behalf of a syndicate of contractors who had been making a great deal of money off the Indian wars.

**ONE OF C.S. FLY'S PHOTOGRAPHS
OF GENERAL CROOK'S NEGOTIATIONS
WITH GERONIMO'S APACHES IN MEXICO, 1886.**

Geronimo's band remained on the warpath for five more months before surrendering to Lt. Charles Gatewood and departing to exile in Florida. Despite Crook's original promise of only a two-year stay, the Chiricahua Apaches remained in Florida for 17 years.

Fly's photos of the Apaches sold well, especially when Mollie gathered them into books. She hit upon the idea of putting his best pictures of the Apaches into a booklet, which she retouched and hand tinted. The book sold well in California, but the photographs never produced the bonanza for which Fly hoped, partly because Geronimo didn't actually surrender at the Mexican canyon. More to the point, Fly sank much of his money into a silver mine venture but wound up with only an empty, 80-foot-deep mine shaft.

He enjoyed a final triumph when he was elected sheriff of Cochise County in 1896, but it wasn't much of a job by then.

The deep silver mines of Tombstone hit the water table,

and the plunging price of silver shut them down. Tombstone began to empty. Fly did help lead a posse which chased three bank robbers into Skeleton Canyon. But the outlaws killed one posse member and critically wounded another before slipping away into Mexico. After a single, undistinguished term as sheriff, Fly returned to private life.

All of his ups and downs, financial losses, and long absences inevitably took their toll on his marriage. Also, there were always strong hints that C.S. lived too much of the Tombstone high life: heavy drinking and long nights at the saloons with partying friends. Mollie remained at home, raising their two adopted children, running both the boardinghouse and the studio, photographing when C.S. was unable to, and finding new ways to sell his work. At one point in 1893, leaving Mollie to operate the studio in the then-dying Tombstone, Camillus moved to the growing settlement of Phoenix. There he opened a second studio, but like so many of his ventures, it soon foundered.

He returned to Tombstone for a time, but both Tombstone and his marriage to the long-suffering Mollie had faded to a shadow of their former selves. The couple separated about 1896, after some 17 years of marriage. He closed his studio in Tombstone and opened another in nearby Bisbee, leaving Mollie behind again in Tombstone. Gradually, his fortunes dwindled and he retired to a ranch at the base of a tall peak in the Chiricahuas. There, he developed a painful bacterial infection of the skin and dwindled toward death — broke and mostly alone. Mollie learned of his illness and sped to his bedside.

He died in 1901, prompting a Tombstone funeral procession he undoubtedly would have loved to photograph. The *Tucson Citizen* observed: "Fly was a genial, whole-souled man, who after his retirement from office, fell by the wayside in Bisbee." The *Tombstone Prospector* noted: "Mr. Fly was a pioneer of Tombstone . . . sharing life's vicissitudes and leaving his survivors to speak the kindest words of him."

Mollie lived on, continuing to run a photography studio

and take pictures of her own, determined to hang on in Tombstone, although it had become nearly a ghost town.

A fire which destroyed her photo gallery in 1912 destroyed many of the Flys' photographs, a terrible blow to future historians. Fortunately, not all of their work had been warehoused in the destroyed studio, and those photographs survived.

Mollie Fly moved to Southern California, where she remained until her death. She continued to protect and promote the photographs both she and her husband took in Tombstone, when they were witnesses to the legendary West. Many of Fly's photographs, some showing fire and water damage from previous fires, today appear in almost every book about that period. (More than one portrait in other chapters of this book bear the notation of Fly's Studio.)

But in the end, despite all his dreams and Mollie's efforts, the fame and fortune that C.S. Fly sought largely eluded him. In his final, lonely years, he understood, no doubt, that expression of fierce sorrow he captured on Geronimo's face.

CHAPTER NINE

IKE CLANTON

*Rustler, thief, murderer, and coward,
Ike Clanton violated
even the bonds of brotherhood and friendship.
How fitting, then, that he died without glory,
cut down by a friend's bullet.*

BY LEO W. BANKS

⟹◆⟸

TOMBSTONE DESPERADO IKE CLANTON DIED LIKE THE SORRY outlaw he was one pretty June morning in 1887. Just after breakfast, he rode up to James Wilson's cabin on Eagle Creek, near Clifton, unaware that three Apache County lawmen were inside.

Hearing the approaching hooves, Deputy Sheriff Jonas V. Brighton opened the door and recognized Ike. Knowing that Ike was wanted on cattle-rustling charges, the deputy told him to throw up his hands, but Ike wheeled and spurred his mount, drawing his long Winchester from its scabbard and menacing the lawmen.

Brighton sighted and fired. Striking Ike under the left arm, the fatal bullet tore through his chest and out the other side, toppling him from his saddle.

He had escaped the sworn revenge of the celebrated Wyatt Earp but could not outrun Jonas Brighton, a mail-order cop with a rifle and a shady past.

Of all the characters in the Tombstone saga, Joseph Isaac "Ike" Clanton stands unredeemed. Johnny Ringo's memory has been filtered through a veil of romance. Curly Bill Brocius, in spite of his badness, was occasionally described as a decent fellow — when sober. But Ike is remembered without such window dressing.

Ike was all bad, a drunken, tobacco-stained braggart and lover of fast horses, an incessant talker and practiced liar who would do anything to turn a silver dollar, even betray his friends. Much of his 40 years was devoted to making and escaping trouble.

Not only that, but as Wyatt's wife, Josie, once noted, he chewed with his mouth open. "Ike was an entirely unlovely person in my eyes," she wrote in her memoirs.

Ike Clanton, who once boasted that he "never made a track with one foot that he didn't cover up with the other," was born in Callaway County, Missouri, in 1847, one of seven children of family patriarch Newman Haynes Clanton.

The Old Man, as he was commonly known, was a Tennessee-born frontiersman who probably took part in the California gold rush in 1850 before moving his family to Texas and signing on to fight for the Confederacy. He didn't wear the uniform with honor, and neither did his first son, John Wesley. Their service records are sketchy, but it appears both men deserted after short stints.

The family roamed. In 1865, they passed through Fort Bowie, Arizona Territory, en route to California. By the early 1870s, they were on the move again, dropping stakes in Arizona's Gila Valley, where Old Man Clanton started a farm and a settlement called Clantonville.

But the town failed, and in 1878, Old Man Clanton and three of his sons moved to the San Pedro Valley, about 14 miles from Tombstone.

There Ike opened a restaurant. Little is known about his short-lived enterprise, although it's hard to imagine his grubby appearance and ruffian ways doing much to attract customers, even in a mining camp. He called his restaurant the Star.

The family's new ranch at Lewis Springs sat in a grassy valley. The location was a prime route for running "wet" cattle up from Mexico. Rustling became the family business, as former Tombstone lawman and Clanton friend Billy Breakenridge noted in his book, *Helldorado*.

JOSEPH ISAAC "IKE" CLANTON

"The Clantons looked after the rustlers' interest on the San Pedro," he wrote, "as a lot of stolen stock was brought from Mexico down the river, and there was no one watching the line for smugglers."

But clipping beef was only part of the Clanton enterprise. In union with the McLaury family, Curly Bill, Ringo, and other Texas cowboys, they formed a mob involved in shootings, robberies, and shakedowns of every sort.

The discord with the Earps grew in steps, the first coming shortly after Wyatt rolled into Tombstone in December, 1879. Billy Clanton, then 17, stole a horse belonging to Wyatt. Ike got into the act a year later in an episode that showed the Territory's rampant corruption and the family's deep involvement in it.

Ike and brother Phineas Fay, nicknamed Phin, managed to get appointed election monitors in the village of San Simon.

The race was for Pima County sheriff, and the Clantons wanted to make sure that their man, incumbent Charlie Shibell, bested Bob Paul, a Wells Fargo employee and a good friend of Wyatt Earp.

In his typescript history of the Clantons on file at the Arizona Historical Society, writer Bob Palmquist stated that Ike and Phin Clanton turned in 106 votes for Shibell and one for Paul — a total of 107 votes in a precinct with only four registered voters. Even after that chicanery was exposed, and long after the family's criminal bent became known, newspapers still portrayed the Clanton boys as upstanding citizens.

The *Arizona Daily Star* called them "fine specimens of the frontier cattle man," describing Billy as "over six feet in height and built in proportion, while Isaac and Phineas are wiry, determined-looking men, without a pound of surplus flesh." The paper said the boys "lived on horse-back and led a life of hardship."

Old Man Clanton's ambush death while on a smuggling run in August, 1881, made Ike the family boss. By that time, his trouble with the Earps was deepening, due largely to a March 15 stagecoach robbery outside Tombstone.

Eager to corral the robbers, Wyatt offered a Ike deal. He wanted Ike to lure the three at-large bandits into a trap. With their arrests, Wyatt would get the glory, raising his stock as a lawman, and in return he'd pass on Wells Fargo's $3,600 reward to Ike.

But word leaked of Ike's betrayal of his highwaymen cronies. Fearing they'd kill him, he began to denounce the Earps loudly and publicly. It was Ike's way of covering his tracks. It backfired. The resulting bitterness led directly to the October 26 showdown.

Ike spent the night before the gunplay working on a tremendous bender and making death threats against the Earps and Doc Holliday. By morning, he was prowling Tombstone with a Winchester and a sidearm, swearing to bring the fight talk to a close.

At one point, he barked at Wyatt, "Fight is my racket, and all I want is four feet of ground to fight on."

But it was just a cheap boast, Ike's specialty. When the two parties met near the O.K. Corral a few hours later, Ike, still unarmed, stood in front of Wyatt and begged for his life. And when the firing became general, he ran like a rabbit, leaving behind little brother Billy, and Tom and Frank McLaury, to die.

Ike filed murder charges against the Earps, but his testimony was fraught with lies and dismissed outright. Unable to win satisfaction in court, he turned to ambush. Ike was almost certainly among the assassins who shot and crippled Virgil Earp as he crossed Tombstone's Allen Street on the night of December 28, 1881.

The finger of suspicion quickly pointed to Ike, since, incredibly, he'd left his sombrero at the ambush site. When Wyatt armed himself with a warrant and set out after his brother's would-be killer, Ike wisely turned himself in to County Sheriff Johnny Behan, a friend and protector.

Seven friendly witnesses swore that Ike was in Charleston the night of Virgil's ambush. As for the incriminating hat, Ike said his enemies had planted it. He was turned loose.

About this time, Ike appeared at the Sierra Bonita Ranch in the Sulphur Springs Valley, hoping to collect on owner Henry Hooker's offer of $1,000 to anyone delivering the head of Curly Bill Brocius. In his book, *Wyatt Earp: Frontier Marshal*, Stuart Lake described Ike galloping up, and in front of Hooker and foreman Billy Whelan, rolling "from a sack the head of a swarthy individual whose death was of recent date."

Ike claimed it was Curly Bill and demanded the reward money. But Hooker and Whelan, who knew Bill too well, laughed at Ike and sent him on. Lake wrote that the head was later established to be that of an "itinerant Mexican with a curly thatch whom Ike had killed in his scheme to collect the cattleman's cash."

But Ike's role as the Earps' chief nemesis wasn't yet

**NEWMAN H. "OLD MAN" CLANTON,
IKE'S FATHER.**

complete. The back-shooting death of Morgan Earp on March 18, 1882, also bore Ike's stamp. Although Ike was not the shooter, Wyatt held him directly responsible and put Ike's name on the list of men he fixed to kill in retaliation.

Wyatt almost got the chance. Two nights after Morgan's murder, as the Earps arrived in Tucson on the westbound train, Ike was at the Southern Pacific Railroad yard with Frank Stilwell, one of the suspected triggermen in Morgan's death.

Again Ike fled, just moments before Wyatt, Holliday, and other posse members riddled Stilwell with bullets. Wyatt and his men then spent several hours turning downtown Tucson upside down in a fruitless search for the slippery villain.

Late in 1882, Ike and brother Phin moved to Apache County, 200 miles north of Tombstone. But nothing changed. The two Clantons, along with brother-in-law Ebin Stanley, were involved in all manner of crimes — from land swindles and shootings to the old standby of cattle rustling.

Over the years, the three racked up an impressive list of

Apache County indictments for grand larceny, usually involving the suspicious marking and branding of calves. In November, 1886, they coldly murdered Isaac Ellinger while attempting to take over his ranch. When Ike rode up to Wilson's cabin that fateful day in June, 1887, he was a wanted man.

And a wanted man that Jonas Brighton knew well. It seems that before he became a mail-order lawman, Brighton himself stole cattle under the nickname Rawhide Jake, riding with the Clantons and claiming them as his friends.

Only the year before, in May, 1886, after Ike shot and wounded a man over a cribbage game in a Springerville saloon, he had fled to Brighton's house. Lawmen caught up with him there, but released him when it was determined that the victim, Pablo Romero, had started the gunplay.

Why Rawhide Jake — whose work also sent Phin Clanton to prison — turned from Ike's friend into his deadly pursuer is unclear. Most likely, money persuaded him.

Some believe Brighton worked for the state cattleman's association, a group that wanted Ike as dead as they could make him. Late in life, Brighton himself claimed he was actually working undercover for Wells Fargo. It's ironic that Ike Clanton, who once planned to turn in his pals for a $3,600 Wells Fargo reward, himself died for a price, shot by a one-time friend.

CHAPTER TEN

CURLY BILL BROCIUS

*Curly Bill was mean with a gun, and
plenty of folks wanted him dead.
He had been rumored dead once before,
only to turn up alive and kicking.
Perhaps he really made it to Mexico. Or perhaps
Wyatt Earp really was the death of him.*

BY LEO W. BANKS

⟫◆⟪

THE MIXTURE WAS POSITIVELY EXPLOSIVE: WILD ARIZONA Territory in the early 1880s and debonair bandit Curly Bill Brocius, with his unquenchable thirst for whiskey and violence.

The two sizzled with an outlaw chemistry that created a time of terrible lawlessness and provided pulp writers with quantities of gore and ample opportunities for frontier fantasy. In his day, they called Curly Bill everything from a merry murderer and conscienceless scoundrel to the very image of the dime-store hero.

The *Silver City Enterprise*, a New Mexico newspaper, might have best captured the essence of the Curly Bill legend, if not the man, with this description:

"His rude makeup of rough pants stuck in his boots, blue shirt, flaming red necktie and great sombrero added to a bad countenance much that is picturesque. He had a knife in his boot, two six-shooters stuck against his waist and was ready for a frolic any time, even at the risk of his life."

This Texas-born ruffian first rode into Arizona about 1878 while driving a herd of cattle to the San Carlos Apache Reservation. By 1882, according to history's most recited version, he was gunned down by none other than Wyatt Earp himself.

But in those four brief years, it seemed that Curly Bill managed to put himself in the middle of almost every shoot-out in the southern portion of the Territory.

Oddly enough, what first brought Curly Bill to wide public attention was an accident: the shooting death of Marshal Fred White of Tombstone.

The night of October 28, 1880, Curly Bill was leading a band of drunken cowboys through Tombstone, waving his pistol at passersby and daring anyone to start something.

When White attempted to disarm Bill, the drunken outlaw balked, and Wyatt Earp stepped in. He threw his arms around Curly Bill's shoulders just as White grabbed for Bill's gun. The weapon discharged, hitting White in the groin. He died two days later.

Wyatt hurried Bill out of Tombstone, probably saving him from a lynch mob. In part due to Wyatt's testimony, as well as White's own dying declaration that the shooting was an accident, a Tucson court allowed Bill to go free. But his penchant for trouble guaranteed that more confrontations with the Earps would come.

Just nine weeks after White's death, Bill and a cowboy friend went on a spree that became famous throughout the West, according to Casey Tefertiller, author of *Wyatt Earp, The Life Behind the Legend*. Bill and his partner stormed into a Mexican dance hall in Charleston, not far from Tombstone, with guns drawn.

"Strip, every one of you!" Bill barked to the shocked crowd. When they complied, he turned to the band and said, "Now, strike up a tune!"

At that, everyone in the room began to dance naked. The "mad fandango," as Tefertiller called it, went on for a half hour before Bill and his cohort were chased from town by lawmen. The next morning, Bill was three miles away in Contention and still drunk. Along with his cowboy friend, he stormed into the church during a crowded Sunday service and ordered the preacher to dance.

"Come right down," Bill said to the preacher. "It shan't cost you a cent, and Pete, my Christian friend, will provide the music. Now dance a jig and see if you can't discount Solomon in all his glory."

Tefertiller said the preacher realized his protests were pointless and danced before Bill's gun. The spree continued the following night, when Bill and his boys captured Tombstone's Alhambra Saloon and galloped through the streets firing pistols.

Such incidents drew wide publicity and became part of Bill's growing legend. He was already well-known around El Paso, where he was involved in a fatal stage holdup, and in southern New Mexico, around Shakespeare. He was considered a dangerous drunkard who enjoyed shooting quarters from between the fingers of anyone willing to hold them.

But not everyone found him loathsome. Tefertiller recorded the recollections of a Shakespeare, New Mexico, woman who thought him a bit of charmer. When Bill arrived at Emma Muir's home at supper time, her mother offered to set him a plate. But he declined.

"Thanks, ma'am, but somebody might see me here, and it would go hard with you," Curly Bill said. "I have a clean flour sack and I would sure appreciate it if you put some of those biscuits in it. I haven't any money, but I'll drop by some time to pay you."

Bill's reputation followed him into Arizona, where his trade was cattle rustling. At that time, huge ranches sprawled across the Mexican border states of Sonora and Chihuahua. Bill and his gang, which included Johnny Ringo, Ike and Billy Clanton, Frank Leslie, and Joe Hill, boasted that they could shotgun a thousand head up from Mexico in a single night.

The gang made its hideout in a mining camp called Galeyville, tucked away in the canyons of the Chiricahua Mountains, 60 miles northeast of Tombstone. The safety of this robbers' roost allowed Bill and his band to operate with near impunity in San Simon, San Pedro, and Sulphur Springs valleys.

Tom Thornton, a Galeyville hotel keeper, thought Bill's reputation as a desperado was mostly a creation of newspapers, but he did acknowledge that Bill was quarrelsome when when drunk. Thornton said that when Curly Bill ate at his restaurant, Bill would place a pistol on either side of his plate and order everyone else in the room to stay put until he was done eating. Even when he passed out, face down on the table, no one in the room dared move.

In Galeyville in May, 1881, an incident occurred that, for a time at least, had peace-loving Arizonans believing that Curly Bill was dead, felled in a shoot-out. As it turned out, reports of his death were exaggerated, but not by much.

Bill was in a saloon drinking when cowboy-rustler Jim Wallace threatened Deputy Sheriff Billy Breakenridge. Bill, who fancied himself one of the lawman's pals, demanded that Wallace apologize. The *Arizona Weekly Star* reported that Bill, who was "desirous of increasing his record as a man killer," called Wallace out. But Wallace shot first, putting a ball through Bill's neck as he stepped through the saloon doors.

Due to the wound's severity, word quickly spread that Curly Bill was finally dead. No such luck.

As the *Star* reported: "Although the wound is considered very dangerous, congratulations at being freed from this dangerous character are now rather premature, as men of his class usually have a wonderful tenacity of life."

Bill proved that last remark two months later, when he and a band of about 50 cowboys ambushed a pack train of Mexican smugglers in Skeleton Canyon in the Peloncillo Mountains on the Mexican border, killing four of the smugglers. The incident drew a strong protest from officials of the Mexican government and threats of action from Arizona Gov. John J. Gosper. But nothing came of it.

By late March, 1882, Curly Bill's time in Arizona had ended, but historians have never firmly established what happened to him. Most accept as truth Wyatt Earp's account — that he killed Curly Bill in a shotgun battle at Iron Springs, retaliation for Bill's supposed involvement in the murder of Morgan Earp.

The night of March 18, 1882, Morgan was shooting pool at Bob Hatch's Tombstone saloon. Suddenly the window behind Morgan shattered, and a bullet took him down. He died within the hour. Wyatt believed that Curly Bill Brocius was one of his brother's killers.

Just days after Morgan's death, Wyatt and several companions galloped west out of Tombstone to a cottonwood-shaded watering hole in the Whetstone Mountains to take their revenge.

As the *Tombstone Epitaph* told it, Earp's party of six men dismounted and were walking toward the springs when Bill and his gang of nine cowboys opened fire.

"My horse reared and tugged at the bridle in such a wild fashion that I could not regain the saddle," Earp said later. "I reckoned that my time had come. But if I was to die, I proposed that Curly Bill at least should die with me."

So intense was the fire from Curly Bill's men that Wyatt's coat was shredded by bullet tears. One bullet ricocheted off his saddle horn and another struck the heel of his boot. But not a single slug penetrated his body. As Earp's men fled in retreat, Wyatt stayed to finish Curly Bill with a shotgun blast.

"His chest was tore open by the big charge of buckshot," Earp said. "He yelled like a demon as he went down."

Doubts about the truth of Bill's death were immediate. Tefertiller wrote that the cowboys, after carrying Bill off and burying him on a nearby ranch, began a campaign of misinformation in which they claimed their leader was still alive. The motive, most likely, was to prevent Wyatt from collecting the $1,000 reward on Bill's head.

The outlaw rogue was such good newspaper copy that his death drew notice as far away as the *San Francisco Exchange*:

"So Curly Bill has at last been gathered in. Arizona tourists will miss the cheerful presence of Bill when they stop overnight at Tombstone or Tucson. His merry pranks were the talk of the town and the newspapers. His playful exhibition of his skill with the pistol never failed to delight those communities which the peripatetic William favored with his presence."

Some believe the best evidence that Bill finally fell before Wyatt's shotgun came in the silence that followed the Iron Springs affair. Simply put, Curly Bill wasn't heard from again.

But his legend never succumbed. In the ensuing years, reports continued to surface that Curly Bill Brocius was very much alive, spotted in Benson, Galeyville, and Safford in Arizona, then in Wyoming and Texas.

In the 1920s, a respected Bisbee citizen swore that he'd just visited Curly Bill in Chihuahua, Mexico, where, he said, the ex-outlaw had become a prosperous rancher and father of 11 children.

No tale was too outrageous, including one that Bill never made it to his confrontation under the cottonwoods with Wyatt because he'd already been shot off his horse by Doc Holliday and buried at Boothill.

Legends never die as easily as the real man. Rest assured, Curly Bill is not at Boothill, but it's likely that some of the men he brought to ruin are.

They say the girls at Tombstone's famed Bird Cage Theatre used to sing a simple refrain:

> When Curly Bill came over the hill
> All the way from Galeyville
> Good-bye, my lover, good-bye.

CHAPTER ELEVEN

ALLEN ENGLISH

*Tombstone's celebrated lawyer earned and lost
more than one fortune with a flamboyance he
was known for, in and out of the courtroom.
Whether practicing law or drinking,
witty Allen English made the bar his own.*

BY LEO W. BANKS

━━━◆◆◆━━━

ALLEN ROBERT ENGLISH SELDOM BLEW A BREATH THAT wasn't drenched in bourbon or wit. He knew Shakespeare and was intimate with the works of great poets and the philosophy of the ancient Greeks. If summoning the memory of literary giants, or that of his mother, or of anyone else's mother, might convince a jury of the wrongs done his client, English would summon away.

He was known as Tombstone's greatest lawyer. A difficult title to earn in a town where reputations were made more with bullets than brains, but then, English's colorful life demands to be remembered.

He was born in Saginaw, Michigan, in July, 1858. He was barely past 20 when he came to Tombstone, rented a room in a not-so-lavish boardinghouse, and took a job in the mines.

Some writers claim English graduated from the University of Michigan law school at age 19, while others say it was the University of Virginia. But neither school has any record of him attending or graduating.

What is unquestionably true is that shortly after landing in Tombstone, he befriended influential lawyer Marcus Aurelius Smith. Later a congressman and senator, Smith brought English into his law firm as junior partner.

The office of Smith and Goodrich was on Fourth Street,

between Toughnut and Allen streets, a stretch of unassuming adobes populated mostly by lawyers and dubbed Rotten Row.

In an interview transcript on file at the Arizona Historical Society, English's son, Roy, said English met his first wife in Michigan when she handed him a long-stemmed red rose. He was a lover of roses, and the gesture captured his heart.

The two were married August 7, 1881, on the banks of the San Pedro River in Charleston, a mill town just outside Tombstone. The ceremony was performed by Jim Burnett, a justice of the peace known for making law at the point of a shotgun.

But English's wife found his drinking intolerable and divorced him. So did his second wife, and the third. These unions produced three sons — Roy, Bryan, and Robert — and much heartache. But similar failure didn't follow English in his professional life.

By 1881, he was Tombstone's justice of the peace. In 1887 and 1888, and again in 1891 and 1892, he served as district attorney of Cochise County. But English made his name as a defense attorney.

"He was a very quick man," Roy English recalled. "He had the law right in his hands. Many lawyers used to go to him to find out things about the law."

Those who watched him work attributed his riveting courtroom presence, in part, to his physical bearing. Historian C.L. Sonnichsen, writing in *Billy King's Tombstone*, offered this description:

"Six feet two and built of roomy lines, he seemed to have been created to fill the shoes of a general or a judge. Providence had blessed him with an abundance of hair, and he did not despise the gift. He allowed his thatch to grow luxuriantly over his ears and down his neck, and he cultivated a big mustache and a noble set of chin whiskers which he kept carefully trimmed to a point."

That look was coupled with a speaking style that Sonnichsen said became "the wonder of every hardy Westerner who heard him."

Even drunk, English could fetch a jury to the brink of tears, throw a gleam of joy into their wide-open eyes, then fill them with passionate outrage at the wrongs done his client. And when he was finished, he'd add a down-home touch by leaning over the railing and saying to a juror he knew from the mines, "Give me a chew of tobacco, Jim."

ALLEN ENGLISH, CIRCA 1880.

One of the most-repeated English stories occurred in 1900, when he was considered a lock to win the job of U.S. commissioner.

English had his belly to the rail at Billy King's when he got involved in an argument that led to a bet — English was adamant that it wouldn't rain on San Juan's Day, and if it did, he'd strip and stand under a waterspout out on the street.

English lost his bet, got himself good and naked, and went outside to keep his word. Somehow, a picture of the famed defense lawyer cavorting under the waterspout made its way to Washington, and English was never offered the commissioner's appointment.

Another oft-told incident occurred during English's defense of accused murderer Wiley Morgan. At a midday break in the 1902 trial, English followed his custom and hurried down the street to a saloon, where he proceeded to punish a whiskey bottle.

When it came time to return to afternoon court, he dropped onto the saloon floor for a nap. According to Sonnichsen, King ordered his horse and wagon from the O.K. Corral, and with the help of a few cronies, loaded the bleary-eyed lawyer aboard.

It didn't look good for Morgan when English staggered

into court and grabbed the jury rail to steady himself before beginning. But his closing argument consisted of some of the finest oratory English had ever given, and Morgan got off.

The flamboyant lawyer's long list of friends did not include the Territory's judges. He clashed with many of them, often using his tongue as a sword.

He once appeared in court so wobbly that a judge fined him $25 for contempt, whereupon English barked, "Your honor, $25 won't pay for half the contempt I have for this court!"

The *Tombstone Epitaph's* centennial edition tells of English working a murder trial before Judge Alfred Lockwood, who spotted the defense lawyer's drunkenness and halted the proceedings for the day.

In spite of Judge Lockwood's warning to never again disgrace the court that way, English showed up drunk in court the next morning. When the furious Lockwood sentenced him to 30 days, English summoned his powers of persuasion and launched into a 15-minute oration that left tears in the eyes of both the jury and the judge.

"Enough, Mr. English, enough," Lockwood said. "I hereby reduce your sentence to 15 days."

On his way out of the courtroom, the "contemptuous Mr. English," as the newspapers often called him, mumbled to a friend, "Well, I talked my way out of half of it anyway."

His ability to persuade earned English the most elegant home in Tombstone, across the street from St. Paul's Episcopal Church, and outrageous sums of money.

The Santa Fe Railroad once offered him the job of company lawyer at $25,000 a year, with the request that he quit drinking.

"What!" English hollered. "Give up my rights! Hell, no!"

Whatever money English earned was quickly and garishly spent. In his book, *Brewery Gulch: Frontier Days of Old Arizona*, pioneer Joseph Chisholm tells of English scoring a $70,000 fee and heading to New York on a spree.

"He bought a Mexican caballero suit and sawed-off

TOMBSTONE'S COCHISE COUNTY COURTHOUSE,
BUILT IN 1883 WHEN TOMBSTONE WAS THE COUNTY SEAT,
IS TODAY A STATE HISTORIC PARK.

bolero jacket, silk pants gored below the knee and spangled with bells, and got a two-story sombrero covered with enough bullion to give a government mule a headache," Chisholm wrote.

Upon his return, English strolled into Billy King's and asked for a calculation of his bar tab. He slapped down what it took to cover it, then announced that he'd exhausted his fortune and could he borrow some scratch for another round?

English could always find a friend at the next stool. He was enormously popular, never more so than during his 1892 campaign for district attorney against one of the few men who could stand with him drink for drink, William C. Staehle. Known as the Colonel, Staehle was such an accomplished boozer that his middle initial came to stand for "Corkscrew."

The two men were friends and decided to barnstorm the

county together in a political road show that drew excited voters at every stop. On the eve of the campaign's close, the candidates encountered a normally dry creek rushing full with runoff, forcing them to spend the night short of their scheduled stop at Fort Huachuca.

When addressing the voters the next day, English told of being stopped at the unnamed creek, and said he'd christened it in honor of his opponent.

"I have called it Staehle Creek," he said. "You must realize how appropriate the name is. Arizona creeks and the Colonel are alike — full every night and dry next morning."

The crowd roared, and Staehle knew that in a tight race, a quip such as that could turn the tide. Chisholm wrote that on the ride back to Bisbee, Staehle racked his brains searching for an equally resounding line.

At the final rally in Bisbee, English told the same story and got the same response. But this time Staehle was ready for him. Chisholm wrote that Staehle thanked his opponent for his thoughtfulness in naming the creek after him, and said:

"But I couldn't ask you for a single vote if I did not repay that touching act of friendship. So today when we crossed the grand old San Pedro River I christened it English River — because it's always full."

The crowd collapsed in laughter. Staehle went on to win by four votes.

But high living eventually caught up with the contemptuous Mr. English. He spent his last years in Bisbee, dissolute and drunk, living on a $200-a-month pension charitably provided by a mining company he'd done some work for.

"Dad let everything slip through his fingers," Roy English said. "He didn't value anything, I don't think, very much. But he let all his property and land go to taxes. He didn't want to bother with it when he got old."

The *Bisbee Daily Review* reported that English stopped practicing law in the mid-1920s, but maintained an office in town. There he would greet old friends and dispense advice to visiting young lawyers, who came by the scores to shake his hand.

The final public images of English are sad indeed. The *Review* wrote that in the summer of 1926, a lingering illness confined him to a wheelchair, and early in September he was taken to the county hospital at Douglas, near death and a pauper. The man who loved Shakespeare and long-stemmed roses died there on September 7, 1926.

A friend and court stenographer named Marie saw to his burial at Bisbee's Evergreen Cemetery. At the time, he was called one of the most brilliant lawyers the Arizona bar ever produced, but today his gravesite is unmarked.

What a far cry from his glory days in Tombstone, where English, the saloon back-slapper and renowned wag, once stepped through the bat-wing doors of the Crystal Palace, spotted the full moon and declared, "Oh moon, thou art full! But you ain't a damn bit ahead of me!"

CHAPTER TWELVE

TOMBSTONE'S TRIALS BY FIRE

The Arizona desert heat may have seemed
"hotter than the blazes," but Tombstone literally
became an inferno more than once.
The sturdy townspeople not only survived,
they did something about it.

BY   CHERYL   BAISDEN

———◆———

THE HAUNTING CREAK OF THE WOODEN SIGNS AT THE O.K. Corral and the Crystal Palace Saloon echoed through the streets of Tombstone. A fierce wind gathered sand from the desert floor and created whirling dust devils, forcing the likes of Wyatt Earp and Doc Holliday to shield their eyes with their weathered black hats while sauntering from one gambling hall to another.

The year was 1881, and Tombstone had come a long way since its founding in 1879, when silver was discovered in the craggy Dragoon Mountains and desolate valleys below. At first, only makeshift tents dotted the rough roadways, but within a few months, permanent wooden buildings, linked by parched plank walkways, staked their claim in the desert.

Life in Tombstone was playing out in a steady rhythm. Miners trudged off to work each morning, greeting the dawn with the same exhaustion they harbored at twilight. Merchants measured out lengths of cloth, weighed bags of flour and sides of beef. Smoky saloons and fancy restaurants, dance halls and cathouses — all catered day and night to the insatiable appetites of high-strung gamblers, shady transients, and upstanding townsfolk alike.

TOMBSTONE FIRE DEPARTMENT, CIRCA 1883, POSSIBLY PHOTOGRAPHED BY C.S. FLY.

On Sundays the pure voices of the church choir some-how managed to harmonize with the raunchy tones of saloon pi-anos. As a thriving community, Tombstone offered some protection from the harsh struggle of frontier life.

Inscriptions on a number of Boothill graves attested to the fact that such protection did not always mean from each other. And the struggle against forces of nature was almost more than residents could handle when fire first struck the town on June 22, 1881.

The summer heat had risen to 100°F. in the shade at 3:30 P.M. on that late June afternoon. Thompson and Alexander, proprietors of the Arcade Saloon on Allen Street, were trundling a barrel of condemned whiskey out to the roadside.

Standing on the wooden sidewalk, they carefully removed the barrel's plug to measure the remaining liquor. When Alexander inadvertently dropped the gauge into the cavernous container, an eager bartender rushed to help and began fishing for the device. Clenched in his teeth was a smoldering stogie. A lit cigar and volatile whiskey fumes. . . .

Suddenly, with an almost indiscernible flash of light, the fumes ignited, and the town quaked under an explosion.

"It came like a clap of thunder, and fire spread with a velocity equaled only by a burning prairie in a gale," the *Tombstone Epitaph* reported days later.

In less than three minutes, the flames were licking at nearby buildings, and the "city of Tombstone was startled by the cry of 'Fire!' In a few minutes, the streets were crowded by people rushing to the scene," the *Arizona Gazette* reported. "The fire spread with wonderful rapidity and inside of 20 minutes had extended over a space of four blocks. The buildings, mostly wood, with but a few adobes between, had produced intense heat, which generated a stiff breeze."

Fed by the wind, sun, and parched wood, the fire quickly encompassed the center of town, sweeping along Allen Street to Fifth. As members of the volunteer bucket brigade attempted to douse the flames with the few available buckets of water, others organized citizens to demolish awnings and porches in an unsuccessful attempt to halt the blaze's steady progress.

With the fire already licking at the board walls of the Safford Hudson Bank on Fifth Street, the bank manager dashed inside, placing cash in the inner safe and frantically tossing ledgers into the dirt road. Next door, at Fitzhenry's Grocery, a human assembly line rapidly passed food and supplies to the safety of the street, while miners and firemen wielded axes and ropes in a struggle to tear down the wooden porch. Still, the wind pushed the fire inexorably on toward Fremont Street.

Armed with wet blankets and buckets of water, firefighters barred the blaze from crossing Fremont, but two red-light district blocks were engulfed and destroyed. A series of vacant lots finally quelled the fire's spread. On the other side of Allen Street, everything between Fifth and Sixth streets was destroyed before the fire reached an alley.

By 6 P.M., the conflagration had finally burned itself out.

The very next morning, amid ash and mud and charred rubble, owners of the 66 destroyed buildings were telegraphing for new stock, and carpenters were hard at work rebuilding the devastated town. Within a month, Tombstone rose from the ashes.

Although Tombstone residents suffered a $300,000 loss in the inferno, only one injury was recorded. Volunteer fireman George Parsons fell from the balcony of a house while dismantling the structure. According to Tombstone historian Ben Traywick, Parsons' helmet saved him from death, although he did require extensive facial surgery.

How had Tombstone survived? A permanent frontier town needs a fire department, and a foresighted group of businessmen and miners had founded the Tombstone Volunteer Fire Company in early 1881. This memorable June day was the fire company's first experience with a blaze.

"They were protecting their own interests, so they were always on alert for a fire," Traywick said. "In a town like Tombstone, where the sun could dry out a piece of wood in a few days, and just about everything was made of wood, fire was the worst possible threat."

The fire company began as a bucket brigade, with splintered wooden pails filled with water stationed strategically around the town. Present-day fire Capt. Joseph Perotti Jr. said that with the only well situated a mile away, successfully dousing a blaze took precision and a lot of luck.

"Of course, we did have a soda and acid fire wagon from the very start, but even when the pipeline was laid, in late 1881, there wasn't enough water pressure to make it work," he explained.

So, despite a public water supply, when a second fire erupted on May 25, 1882, Tombstone was still far from prepared for such an emergency.

At 3 P.M., flames mysteriously began licking at the bathroom walls of the Tivoli Saloon on Allen Street near Fifth. By the time the alarm sounded, the fire had engulfed the Tivoli and was spreading along the packed clothesline of an adjoining Chinese laundry.

"In less than 15 minutes, the entire space between Fourth

TOMBSTONE FIRE HOSE CREW, CIRCA 1890.

and Fifth streets and Allen and Toughnut streets was one steaming, smoking, blazing mass of desolation and ruin," the *Epitaph* reported.

Armed with two horse-drawn hose carts hooked to the town's limited water supply, firefighters struggled to douse the flames jumping across Allen Street, but the intense heat forced them to shift their efforts elsewhere.

While they fought on in another quarter, the flames reached the Fourth Street Gun Shop. "Here a scene was presented, magnificent in its fierce grandeur. A large quantity of powder was stored in the cellar, and other explosive materials were in the store. Here, as soon as the flames were communicated to the combustibles, a wild scene presented itself. The loud bursting of cartridges . . . added to the shouting of the men and the screams of the women," the *Epitaph* reported.

During the explosion, the blaze swelled to engulf the town's four central blocks, bounded by Fourth, Sixth, Fremont, and Toughnut streets. Firefighters and citizens began to spread gunpowder in strategic spots to destroy buildings and create vacant lots that they prayed would halt the blaze.

Although their efforts failed to alter the fire's course, a weak but steady spray of water prevented the flames from crossing Sixth, Fremont, and Toughnut streets. But along Fourth Street, the flames were not quelled until they swept across the western side of the street and engulfed 11 additional buildings.

The total damage was even greater than it was the year before. One unidentified body was recovered from the Cosmopolitian Hotel, and a number of firefighters and residents were injured by falling walls, flying debris, and intense heat. This blaze destroyed 116 properties valued at $500,000.

By morning, Tombstone had once again begun the task of rebuilding, but this time with two important changes: Many of the new structures were rebuilt with adobe rather than wood, and the Huachuca Water Company was organized, creating a million-gallon reservoir 21 miles from town.

With a seven-inch pipeline capable of delivering 45,000 gallons of water an hour, the system could send water to fire hydrants at a pressure of 160 pounds to the square inch. For the first time in its short history, Tombstone was capable of fighting a fire, assured that a stream of water from a medium nozzle could reach a height of 260 feet with enough force to easily knock down a miner's cabin.

Two months later, on July 21, 1882, Tombstone's new preparations faced their first test when the town's fire bell sounded at 11:10 P.M.

Expecting the worst again, "a scene of wild confusion prevailed," the *Epitaph* reported. "Women with bare feet and scanty clothing were darting from the burning building, excited men jostled each other hither and thither, furniture was strewn on the streets, law books went flying through the air, costly tableware was trampled underfoot and everything was chaos and hopelessness."

Although the flames reached 50 feet high and engulfed a miner's house and attached restaurant at Fourth and Toughnut streets, the blaze was extinguished in 20 minutes as firefighters directed their new water supply in two streams, one from Fourth Street, the second from Toughnut.

"Basically, what was learned in the two major fires in Tombstone was that a desert town is probably nature's weakest spot when it comes to the threat of fire," Perotti said. "You've heard of trial by fire? Well, that's what our first firefighters went through here. Since that time, our natural resources have improved, and our firefighting equipment and skills are top-notch. We haven't had a fire of real note since 1882."

CHAPTER THIRTEEN

REV. ENDICOTT PEABODY

*This educated, cultured man of the cloth
from back East
went toe to toe with Tombstone's bullies and
rustlers — even another pastor.*

BY DON DEDERA

———◆◆———

"**A**PACK OF LIES AUTHENTICATED BY A LONG, GRAY beard." Such was the wry judgment upon certain memories by the widely published Arizona author, John Myers Myers. He wrote much factual history of the West in general, and of Tombstone in particular. Through it all, he nursed a healthy skepticism of the testimony of eyewitnesses, especially old-timers. Human memory, opined Jack Myers, couldn't be trusted for one day, let alone a century.

Tolstoy considered history "a wonderful thing, if only it were true," and Napoleon dismissed it as "a fable agreed upon."

Fair enough, when dealing with a place such as Tombstone in its heyday, largely populated by liars, horse thieves, tinhorn gamblers, gunfighters, and saloon dames.

But one wonders what we should make of the conflicting eyewitness versions of the style and behavior of Endicott Peabody, the Boston blue-blood vicar of Tombstone's St. Paul's Episcopal Church.

Today, tiny St. Paul's ranks as Arizona's oldest standing Protestant church. With room for only a hundred worshipers, the sanctuary is open daily for quiet meditation. Picturesque St. Paul's would seem far removed from controversy. Yet historical questions persist.

Tombstone was in full-throated roar on Saturday night, January 28, 1882, when Reverend Peabody arrived on the stage from Tucson. Certainly he had never seen anything like this in Massachusetts, neither in Old Salem, where he was born, nor in Cambridge, where he graduated from the Episcopal Theological Seminary. Nor, for that matter, in England, where he attended Cheltenham College.

Not exactly a center of piety and worship, Tombstone, as Peabody noted in his memoirs: "Exports from the waning goldfields of California and Australia, in many cases booted out by vigilante committees, arrived to open gambling halls; two of every three buildings in the business district were saloons and gambling dens. The gamblers of Dodge City, at that time an infamous hellhole, moved in masse; an immense red-light district sprang up."

During a nine-year continuous performance, the Bird Cage Theatre never closed its doors. Staged variety, melodrama, chorus, vaudeville, and risqué comedy induced 24-hour thirst slaked by relays of bartenders and showgirls. Real gunfire frequently punctuated make-believe drama. Once, offended by a foot dangling from a box, Buckskin Frank Leslie shot the heel off the boot.

Another time, during a production of *Uncle Tom's Cabin* (as reported by the *Arizona Star*): "Just as Eliza was crossing the icy river, a drunken cowboy in the audience got excited and shot the bloodhound that was pursuing her. After something of a fight, the cowboy was lodged in jail, and the show continued minus one good hound."

Preserved is Peabody's own first impression of Tombstone: "The town contained a great body of men and women unmoral, shameless, and cruel. There was no such thing as public opinion, for the community was unorganized and each person did as he chose to do."

Especially in Tombstone's first months, the Sabbath was just one more day in a week of claim jumping, highway robbery, Apache trouble, and casual murder. In a town where no

**REV. ENDICOTT PEABODY,
CIRCA 1881.**

good deed came easily, church attendance was possibly the most difficult of all. Small knots of the faithful (typically a dozen out of a total population of about 4,000) met in tents, in lodge halls, in schoolrooms, in private parlors.

"Hard to preach," wrote George Parsons in his diary after an 1879 service in a canvas-roofed church. "Dance hall racket in rear. Calls to rally to the Lord do not mingle well with 'hug your gals in the corner.' The place is rather a poor one for divine service." Soon afterward, a storm blew away the canvas.

Another entry in Parsons' diary: "Full house. George Upshire made an ass of himself by coming in drunk. . . . Stood on the steps and cursed."

And on another day, regarding Tombstone's clergy, Parsons groused: "Numskulls and old broken down ministers have charge of spirituality."

But change was on the way. Episcopal churchwomen raised funds with rummage sales. Respectable Tombstone families pledged donations. Work began in 1881 on St. Paul's.

Men of the parish baked adobe bricks in the sun and hewed pine timbers freighted by teams of oxen off the Chiricahua Mountains 50 miles distant.

It fell to young Reverend Peabody to complete this project. And how? Did he really solicit and welcome support from the evil elements of wide-open Tombstone? Did he double dare the wicked brutes who threatened him with violence? And did he duke it out with at least one bully who pushed him too far?

Nearly every historical authority agrees — that is truly what happened. From day one, Peabody circulated among the legitimate business leaders and civic uplifters of Tombstone. But he also ventured across Tombstone's "Dead Line" into the devil's own dens and ingratiated himself with sinners of every sort. In a word, he was immensely popular.

Tall and athletic, at his physical prime in his mid-20s, Reverend Peabody regularly worked out in the local gymnasium. He volunteered to umpire at baseball games and to referee wrestling matches, upon whose outcome the town toughs wagered fortunes. Reverend Peabody also attended horse races, where betting was rife.

According to more than one chronicler, Peabody took on the Methodist minister in a sparring match and won. A manifestly desirable bachelor, Reverend Peabody attracted the attentions of the better class of young Tombstone ladies.

In his diary, George Parsons practically cheered: "Walked home with Peabody and stayed quite a while at his house, smoking and talking. Peabody likes his claret and a good cigar and I don't see why he shouldn't enjoy them, [even] if he is a minister. He is a sensible, manly fellow and I like him very much. [He] is quite an athlete and of magnificent build, weighing nearly 200 pounds, muscles as hard as iron."

Regarding the boxing match with the Methodist preacher, Parsons wrote: "The Methodist will be licked as sure as fate. Both have told me they would box with the other, so sometime after Lent is over I must arrange a battle. What joy. Peabody's a jolly good fellow."

INTERIOR OF ST. PAUL'S EPISCOPAL CHURCH, CIRCA 1884.

Meanwhile, the Lord's work awaited. One of Peabody's predecessors had been humiliated in the outlaw stronghold and river mill town of Charleston, 11 miles to the west. Curly Bill Brocius, ever trigger-happy and on a whisky binge, had shot out the windows of Charleston's one poor church and had forced the hapless preacher to dance a jig at gunpoint.

One Sunday, Peabody went to Charleston and preached a sermon against horse thievery. Offended, a notorious, volatile long roper and cardsharp, Billy Claibourn, warned Peabody never, ever to return. Unfazed, Peabody sent Claibourn a special invitation. And two weeks later Peabody again took the pulpit in Charleston and denounced the evils of gambling.

In *Helldorado*, his classic book of Tombstone recollections first published in 1928, former sheriff's deputy William M. Breakenridge recounts Peabody's daring and unorthodox fundraising methods:

- In a hotel casino, the clergyman introduced himself to

the players in a high-stakes poker game "and asked them for a donation to help build a church." Mine manager E.B. Gage obligingly "counted out about $150 from his pile in front of him, and everybody else in the room followed his example."

• "A musical society . . . conceived of the idea of putting on the comic opera *H.M.S. Pinafore*, although the expense of staging it was very high, as they had to send to San Francisco for their costumes." The play netted $250 for Peabody's church, probably because saloons bought batches of tickets they didn't use.

• "Peabody was known to go into saloons . . . and say, 'Gentlemen, I am going to preach on the evil of gambling Sunday night, and I would like to have you all come to church and listen to it. And by the way, drop some dollars into the collection plate.'"

About the celebrated fistfight, Arizona historian Lester "Budge" Ruffner tells it this way:

> He was fond of boxing and baseball. . . . He pulled no punches either in the ring or the pulpit.
>
> On one occasion he delivered a sermon on cattle rustling (thou shalt not covet thy neighbor's cows), to which an advocate of the art took sour exception.
>
> The individual, who thought he had been personally cited in the cattle rustling sermon, began to confront and harass him. Peabody would attempt to reason and assure him, but the man stepped up his threats. To resolve the conflict short of a second O. K. Corral, Reverend Peabody suggested a boxing match in a local bar. Tickets would be sold to benefit Tombstone's less fortunate. The ruffian, clamoring for a chance to clobber the clergyman, gleefully accepted the challenge. It was no match. Peabody countered with nothing but defensive jabs until his opponent threw his Sunday punch, which

never landed. The reverend's punch was even more potent than his sermon.

With St. Paul's construction completed in July, 1882, Reverend Peabody returned to Massachusetts to found the prestigious college preparatory, Groton School, and served 54 years as its headmaster. One of his students was Franklin Delano Roosevelt, at whose second presidential inauguration the Reverend Peabody invoked the blessing.

Tombstone and Arizona Territory were now part of the past. Reverend Peabody officiated at the baptisms, weddings, christenings, and funerals of the elite of Eastern society. He mentored the nation's religious and political leaders.

On February 16, 1941, nearly six decades after he left Tombstone, the senior reverend returned to deliver a stirring sermon at St. Paul's. Afterward, at a public roundtable, the now supremely dignified gentleman was asked to confirm accounts of his youthful exploits.

"Nothing to it at all!" he thundered. "Never had a fist-fight in my life. Stuff and nonsense!"

To one writer, Peabody went out of his way to discredit "stories of heroism on my part which have found their way into some of the books about Tombstone and which are indeed wholly legendary."

Interestingly, though, this same sympathetic writer wrote an article for *Arizona Highways* magazine and included a disclaimer: ". . .[Peabody] denied that professional gamblers and saloon keepers had contributed to help build the church. One member of the gathering, whose mother had been a member of the Ladies Guild of the historic church, refreshed his memory on that point by recalling that the gamblers and saloon keepers had contributed generously to make bazaars and theatricals possible to raise money."

So there you have it — the ecclesiastical enigma of old Tombstone. When young, was Endicott Peabody the two-fisted pastor with a righteous zeal and a good right hook? Or, as he much later in life insisted, a proper Christian, ever willing to play peacemaker and turn the other cheek?

If you can't trust an Episcopal pastor to remember — whether his bow to a pretty girl, his occasional glass of claret and fraternal cheroot, his courageous challenge to Billy Claibourn, his sparring duel with the Methodist preacher, or his knockdown slugfest with Tombstone's town bully — then whom can you trust?

CHAPTER FOURTEEN

SOILED DOVES & SHADY LADIES

*Accepted by many of that day
as a practical service,
denounced by some as great wickedness,
prostitution in Tombstone brought most of the
first women to a new frontier society.*

BY DEAN SMITH

———❦———

S PRINGING UP LIKE DANDELIONS ON AN APRIL LAWN, THE
good-time ladies of Tombstone were already cheerfully
in business when the only walls in the boisterous new
mining camp were still made of canvas.

The miners welcomed these women with open arms and
open pocketbooks, and they enjoyed the exalted status of
celebrities — at least until wives and other "decent" women
started trickling into town. But throughout the decade of the
1880s, the madams and their girls made more than their share
of history in the colorful saga of "the town too tough to die."

In the starkly male society of frontier mining camps, a
touch of femininity was a proven marketing ploy. The prostitutes
brought a measure of civilization to the Tombstone camp, im-
porting the first pianos, the fanciest furniture, the latest fash-
ions, the finest wines, and the first cigarettes that many of the
grizzled residents had ever seen. Some of the "soiled doves," as
local newspapers often called them, cared for the sick and injured and collected money to bury ill-fated gunmen. But just as
many of them were the dregs of humanity — thieves, cheats,
barroom brawlers, and connivers of every stripe.

In those early months of Tombstone's life, when Dodge

City was sending its Earps, Mastersons, Hollidays, and other Old West celebrities to Arizona Territory, ladies of the evening were arriving almost daily. They were on the lookout for new towns that had money flowing freely, were populated primarily by unattached and lonely males, and were far enough removed from the ladies' hometowns to prevent family or friends from dropping in unexpectedly.

Tombstone, Arizona Territory, in 1879 passed all three tests with flying colors.

As canvas tents were replaced by shacks — and the shacks by ornate theaters, saloons, and pleasure houses — the profession of prostitution took on a patina of affluence and near respectability. Nosey Kate, for example, moved into a frame building, assembled a retinue of girls, and was well on the way to becoming rich when an unfortunate incident precipitated her sudden departure from Tombstone.

One evening a cattle buyer strode up to her bar and flashed a roll of bills that had Kate's eyes popping out of her head. As she had often done before, she kept the newcomer swilling whiskey until he was too drunk to notice the knockout drops she had put in his glass.

The late Southwest historian, C.L. Sonnichsen, wrote about what happened next in his book, *Billy King's Tombstone*: "He noted curiously that the walls were in motion and that the floor came up and hit him in the back of the head. He wondered why he was being carried into the back room and hoped they'd let him sleep. Then he felt a hand fumbling for his wallet."

That brought the gentleman abruptly out of his funk, and he fought back. Nosey Kate hadn't figured on this, so in a panic she picked up a beer bottle and landed a mighty blow to his head that ended his resistance. After collecting his valuables, she had his supposedly moribund body dumped in the nearby desert. Miraculously, however, the victim regained consciousness a short time later and brought the police racing to Nosey's Place. But Kate and her partners were long gone by that time.

At the other end of the moral spectrum was China Mary, who controlled Tombstone's Chinatown district. Mary devoted much of her time to nursing sick and injured men back to health in her home — a virtual hospital — and never asked for anything in return. True, she was the major supplier of prostitutes, opium, and other black-market necessities to her clientele, but she was regarded as scrupulously honest and a capable financial manager. She also operated an employment agency that matched Chinese workers with jobs. She guaranteed honest and satisfactory service or she would refund a patron's money.

China Mary made her pile in Tombstone and then went legitimate, returning to China to an arranged marriage and a life of respectability.

Between those two extremes of Tombstone madams were a host of colorful characters representing every shade of morality. All were tough as boot leather — they had to be to survive — but many succumbed occasionally to a sad story from a hungry wayfarer, or grubstaked a prospector who was sure he was about to find a rich lode.

Irish Mag financed a persuasive treasure seeker in a weak moment one night and almost immediately regretted it. But the bread she cast upon the waters came back as three-tiered chocolate cake. The prospector struck it rich and shared the profits with her. Mag banked half a million dollars, which enabled her to retire from her shady business and return to her native Ireland.

There was Madame Moustache, a shrewd manager who never could eradicate the dark hairline above her upper lip. She was the second madam (Blonde Marie was the first) sent to Tombstone by a French syndicate that supplied prostitutes in several Western territories. Her establishment on Allen Street was one of the grandest, and she frequently took her girls on carriage rides through the town, alluringly gowned and coiffed, to advertise her stock in trade.

Another Tombstone character who left her imprint on the

town was Crazy Horse Lil, who tended to get pugnacious when she was drunk, which was quite often.

"I can lick any man in the house!" she would bellow. And sometimes she would prove it.

Lil had her own specialty — staging robberies during which she and her customers were relieved of their money and jewels. Eventually, it was discovered that she was getting her diamonds back from the robbers, along with a sizable portion of the other loot.

MADAME MOUSTACHE, CIRCA 1888.

Big Minnie, a 230-pound bundle of pulchritude in pink tights, served as her own bouncer when a customer got obstreperous. She married little Joe Bignon, proprietor of the Bird Cage Theatre, and the two of them made that Tombstone showplace one of the most notorious dens of iniquity between St. Louis and San Francisco. The Bird Cage, open 24 hours a day for nine years, had 14 gilded cages suspended from the ceiling, in which male patrons (women rarely attended) could dally with their chosen soiled doves while looking down on the merriment below. Things could get rough, though. More than 150 bullet holes were found in its walls when the Bird Cage was refurbished.

One madam was both honest and meticulous. In her University of Arizona master's thesis on Tombstone history, Alice Emily Love tells of Cora Davis (not her real name), who removed a patron's valuables when he drank himself into oblivion. She itemized them in duplicate, placed them in a safe, and returned them with a written inventory when he regained consciousness.

And we must not forget one of the shady ladies with a true heart of gold: Dutch Annie, who sometimes made the pages of Tombstone's *Epitaph* newspaper because of what the editor called "her many charities." She cared for the sick, raised money for orphans, and was often good for a touch from a down-and-outer. So highly was she regarded that when she died, townspeople piled into a thousand buggies (according to the *Epitaph*) to accompany her coffin to her final resting place in Tombstone's cemetery.

In rough-and-ready Tombstone and other Western mining camps, the madams and their ladies of easy virtue often were more than just prostitutes. Especially in the stylish parlor houses, they offered lonely males a social club, a recreation center, and occasionally a confessional experience. The better places demanded that patrons arrive bathed, well-dressed, and sober, and that they refrain from profanity and rough behavior.

But only the most alluring women got to work in such genteel surroundings. Tombstone historian Ben Traywick, in his treatise *Hell's Belles*, described the sordid working conditions of the crib girls who sold their bodies for 10 or 15 minutes to any man with a few coins in his pocket. The cribs (so called because they were about the same size as corncribs) were typically eight by 10 feet, with a chair, table, and narrow bed which was covered with an oilcloth spread to protect it from muddy boots. Apparently, the customers wasted no time in undressing.

Racial prejudice obviously ruled, as shown in one reported fee scale which the crib and street girls could charge: American, $1; French, 75 cents; Mexican, 50 cents; and Negro or Indian, 25 cents. By some reports, the more energetic girls could service 50 or more customers during one night's shift.

It was a brutal and degrading way to earn a living, and the girls risked pregnancy, back-alley abortions, and venereal disease with each new customer. Occasionally, a drunken or jealous patron would inflict bodily harm, and slashings and beatings were hazards of the trade.

Why would a woman choose such a life? According to a poll of 2,000 prostitutes, taken just before the turn of the century by Dr. William Sanger, about a fourth were forced into it by poverty, another fourth by the lure of Western adventure, and the rest by alcoholism, seduction by a friend or relative, or ill treatment by a husband or parents.

Tombstone's soiled doves had a little more choice of lifestyle than those in many other camps because of the presence of the Bird Cage Theatre, dance halls, fancy sa-

CRAZY HORSE LIL, CIRCA 1888.

loons, and other night spots. There were 110 saloons in Tombstone (population 5,000) in 1882, and many of them offered some kind of entertainment for the imbibers. Girls doubled as vaudeville performers, barmaids, musicians, or chorus girls. A young lady who called herself "Lizette, the Flying Nymph" floated above the stage and crowd at the Bird Cage Theatre, suspended from wires, to earn extra money. Those who could sing, act, or dance used those talents to supplement their incomes.

Not all the girls were imported tramps. Traywick tells, for instance, of Benson Annie, a respectable housewife from nearby Benson, who started coming to Tombstone on weekends because of the excitement and liked it so much that she stayed on as a regular employee of one of the red-light district houses. The work paid more than most other jobs available to young ladies of that era, and a few were lucky enough to find romantic liaisons or even husbands in the process.

When Big Nose Kate arrived in Tombstone in 1880, she

supposedly had married the notorious Doc Holliday and lived with him in Texas and Dodge City before they came to Arizona. A young lady of 29 and reasonably good-looking despite her oversize proboscis, she continued in her profession of prostitution in Tombstone while sharing an apartment with Doc. But her excessive drinking and his proclivity for using her as a punching bag brought about a permanent split. Kate banged around Arizona for decades thereafter, and in 1940, just five days before her 90th birthday, she died in the Arizona Pioneers' Home in Prescott.

When the mines started to shut down in the early 1890s, Tombstone began its steady downward slide. The soiled doves moved on to new adventures in new boomtowns. Not that they disappeared entirely, of course. As Arizona Territory mining camps became more stable, the girls were first limited to "tenderloin districts," and finally their professional activities were banned by law. Still, while living on the fringes of acceptable society, the frontier's soiled doves left their imprint in the public's imagination and, in their own way, helped tame the Wild West.

CHAPTER FIFTEEN

JOHNNY RINGO

Sometimes called "King of the Cowboys,"
Johnny Ringo lived life hard and died young.
But if the bullet to his brain
was self-inflicted, why did his body
bear a knife wound as well?

BY   LEO   W.   BANKS

———❖———

HOW FITTING THAT JOHN RINGO WAS FOUND DEAD WITH two wounds in his head, in mysterious circumstances that raised more questions than answers. Having lived a life of myth and extravagant rumor, the famed Tombstone cowboy, cattle rustler, and outlaw couldn't just fade from the scene quietly.

A passing lumberman found Ringo's corpse on the banks of Turkey Creek in southeastern Arizona on July 14, 1882. The first wound, in Ringo's right temple, was a bullet hole probably made by the Colt revolver found clutched in his right hand. That's what the coroner's jury ruled in its decision of death by suicide.

The second wound, in Ringo's forehead, apparently was carved with a knife after his death, perhaps in an aborted scalping attempt. Whoever left behind Johnny's body, though, did not complete the grotesque job.

By calling Ringo's death a suicide, the coroner's jury first noted and then ignored this second wound, leaving others to ask the hard and obvious questions.

If Johnny Ringo committed suicide, why were there no powder burns on his temple?

Who carved that hole in his forehead — and why?

Why was his cartridge belt fastened upside down?

Why were his boots off and his undershirt wrapped around his feet?

Some declare that Ringo was the subject of more extravagant claims and tall tales than even Billy the Kid and Wyatt Earp. As Jack Burrows showed in his 1987 book, *John Ringo: The Gunfighter Who Never Was*, the Ringo myth was entirely false.

He was said to be a brave and honorable gunman, the fastest draw around, a lonely, brooding man who rode with Quantrill's Confederate raiders and was related to the famous Youngers of the Jesse James gang.

Ringo had a way about him, the writers said. He was educated, erudite, thoughtful. "Byronic in mood, appearance and past, with a patrician face," wrote John Myers Myers, one of Doc Holliday's biographers.

Some said Ringo was a college graduate, even an ex-professor at a prestigious Eastern school who kept the shelves of his cabin stocked with the classics, which he read in Latin and Greek to pass time between stints as a cattle rustler.

Supposedly, Ringo was the fallen angel of an aristocratic Southern family, "a man born for better things who stalked the streets of Tombstone, a Hamlet among outlaws," wrote Walter Noble Burns in his 1927 book, *Tombstone*.

Later on, television shows and movies kept Ringo's name alive, even while sometimes rewriting his death. In the movie *Gunfight at the O.K. Corral*, Kirk Douglas as Doc Holliday shot Ringo dead. Actor Lorne Greene even sang a popular song about him:

> Then came down the setting sun
> He practiced with that deadly gun
> And hour on hour I watched in awe
> No human being could match the draw . . . of Ringo.

The raw truth about Ringo is decidedly less romantic. He was a grade-school dropout and a ferocious drunk, possibly

JOHNNY RINGO

psychotic, who in his Arizona days never took part in a single face-to-face gunfight. For the gross mischaracterizations about Ringo, Burrows places at least part of the blame with Ringo's sisters — Fanny, Mary Enna, and Mattie — who spent their lives hiding the family's connections to bad John.

They remained silent in the face of false assertions about their brother, even letting stand the oft-repeated fiction that his real name was Ringgold.

The straitlaced sisters threatened legal action against any writer who veered near the truth, and Mary Enna went to the extent of proclaiming that her brother was a Texas Ranger.

Nice try. But as Burrows pointed out, the truth was that he was arrested by Texas Rangers.

The real Ringo was born on May 3, 1850, in Greenfork, Indiana. At age 14, his father, Martin Ringo, loaded the family — wife Mary, the three sisters, and sons Martin Albert and John — onto a 70-wagon train heading west out of Liberty, Missouri.

Martin hoped the California climate would ease his

suffering from tuberculosis. But his end came a little more than two months into the trip, on July 30, 1864.

Missouri's *Liberty Tribune* published an eyewitness account of Martin's death:

"Just after daylight . . . Mr. Ringo stepped out . . . of wagons as, I suppose, for the purpose of looking around to see if Indians were in sight and his shotgun went off accidentally in his own hands, the load entering at his right eye and coming out the top of his head. At the report of his gun I saw his hat blown up 20 feet in the air and his brains were scattered in all directions."

Mary Ringo wrote in her diary: "May no one ever suffer the anguish that is breaking my heart, my little children are crying all the time and I — oh, what am I to do?"

Mary settled in San Jose, California, hoping to somehow keep her shattered family in place. But John took to drinking, and in 1869, he left for Texas to become a cowboy. He was 19.

The only well-documented cases of men dying at Ringo's hand occurred during his 10 years in Texas. He became a gunman in what was called the "Hoodoo War," a bitter range feud fought in Mason County in the 1870s.

Ringo's first killing came when he and another man known only as Williams rode to the house of one James Cheyney, summoned Cheyney to the porch on friendly pretenses, and shot him dead.

A few days later, Ringo was riding with the Scott Cooley gang, described by one historian as "human coyotes," when they killed a man named Charles Bader. The gang's actual target was Charles' brother, Peter, but it's reasonable to question whether that mattered to Ringo and his leader. Cooley was so cold-blooded that he carried in his pocket the scalp of one of his earlier victims.

Ringo was jailed, escaped, captured again, and eventually indicted for Cheyney's murder. But here Ringo's tracks blur. He served no time for the killing, perhaps by engineering another escape, and wound up fleeing Texas in 1879.

Soon after arriving in Arizona, Ringo found a home in Galeyville, the wild shantytown in the Chiricahua Mountains that was headquarters to the cattle rustlers and cutthroats who terrorized the southern part of the Territory at that time.

These were the notorious outlaw-cowboys whose long and bitter feud with the Earps of Tombstone would come to a head near the O.K. Corral on October 26, 1881.

Although Ringo was not involved in that street fight, he was a frequent and dedicated lawbreaker. In late December, 1879, he shot a man named Hancock in a barroom encounter.

"It appears Ringo wanted Hancock to take a drink, and he refused, saying he would prefer beer," reported the *Arizona Miner*.

"Ringo struck him over the head with his pistol and then fired, the ball taking effect in the lower end of the left ear, and passed through the fleshy part of the neck. Half an inch more in the neck would have killed him. Ringo is under arrest."

Hancock survived. But in the ensuing decades, writers turned the story upside down, reporting that Hancock was killed and that the shooting took place in Tombstone.

Three months later, Ringo wrote to Pima County Sheriff Charles Shibell, saying he couldn't appear before the grand jury looking into the Hancock shooting because "I got shot through the foot and it's impossible for me to travel for awhile [sic]."

Some believe the wound came from the gunman's own gun, a careless accident.

Ringo made news again on August 11, 1881, when the *Tombstone Nugget* published an account of a barroom stunt in Galeyville. It seems that Ringo lost at poker and angrily left the saloon.

"He returned with a companion named David Estes, one being armed with a Henry Rifle and the other with a six-shooter," reported the *Nugget*. "The players were promptly ordered to hold up their hands. And the cowboys proceeded to 'go through' the party, securing in the neighborhood of $500."

Ringo's frequent appearance in saloons fits with the

observation of Wyatt Earp's common-law wife, Josephine, that Ringo had the "whiskey shakes."

Some of his appearances in saloons, though, could be kindly remembered. In his written reminiscence, Arizona rancher A.M. Franklin recalled an incident in which an armed man was doing everything he could to bait Franklin into a fight. Then Ringo entered the picture.

"He [Ringo] heard enough to catch the drift, then he sauntered to the bar . . . slapped down his money and announced, 'All of Franklin's and my friends have a drink.' No one dared insult him by refusing and all had a drink — the obnoxious fellow included."

Franklin told a second story: "At another time a crowd was trying to start something in the store . . . Ringo took in the situation at a glance. Stepping up beside me and slamming his gun on the counter, he remarked, 'If there is going to be a row, I think I would like to be in it.' Everyone suddenly decided they had business elsewhere."

But some of Ringo's deeds, usually committed in conjunction with the cattle-rustling Clanton family and bad man Curly Bill Brocius, were only rumored about, never proved.

Many believe he was in on the killings of storekeepers Ike and Bill Haslett in Eureka, New Mexico, in June, 1881; that he participated in a bloody August, 1881, raid on a Mexican pack train in Skeleton Canyon; and that he helped hold up the Bisbee stage in January, 1882.

Wyatt Earp harbored no doubt that Ringo was among the cowboy conspirators in the ambush shooting that crippled his brother, Virgil, in December, 1881, and in the assassination of younger brother, Morgan, three months later.

Between these two shootings, on January 17, 1882, Ringo called out Doc Holliday on Tombstone's Allen Street. He reportedly held a handkerchief up to Holliday, challenging him to grab one end. Then both were supposed to let go, draw their guns, and shoot it out.

Tombstone diarist George W. Parsons saw the almost-event

and wrote: "Much blood in the air this afternoon. Ringo and Doc Holiday [sic] came nearly having it out with pistols . . . I passed both not knowing blood was up. One with hand in breast pocket and the other probably ready. Earps just beyond. Crowded street and looked like another battle. Police vigilant for once and both disarmed."

Ringo's renown in life was magnified by his death. The *Arizona Daily Star* and the *Tombstone Epitaph* were quick to second the verdict of the coroner's jury. The *Star* headlined its obituary, "The King Of The Cowboys Sends A Bullet Through His Head." And the *Epitaph*, after noting Ringo's frequent talk of suicide, wrote, "The circumstances of the case hardly leave any room for doubt as to his self-destruction."

The *Epitaph* theorized that Ringo had been on an "extended jamboree," lost track of his horse and boots, then wrapped his undershirt around his feet and tried to keep walking. However, heat, liquor, or perhaps an extreme fit of melancholy overcame Ringo, and he sat down against a spreading oak tree and shot himself.

But the murder theorists immediately started picking apart the coroner's hasty findings and positing their own ideas about who killed Ringo and why.

Researchers, writers, and armchair Ringo buffs have since made cases for at least six different killers, including gambler Johnny-Behind-the-Deuce, outlaws Buckskin Frank Leslie and Pony Deal, ranch detective Lou Cooley (not related to Scott Cooley), Doc Holliday, and Wyatt Earp.

Josephine Earp was one who claimed Wyatt shot Ringo, giving a detailed account in her book of how Wyatt tracked and gunned him down. But many found her story suspicious, so the mystery endures. It's likely, more than a century later, that we'll never know the truth about the death of the shiftless "King of the Cowboys," who drank and outlawed himself into a legend far bigger than what he deserved.

CHAPTER SIXTEEN

BAT MASTERSON

*Bat Masterson made his name as a peace officer
on the streets of Dodge City,
but his friendship with Wyatt Earp
did bring him to Tombstone for a time.
Out of loyalty to his friend, Bat would act
against his own better judgment.*

BY LEO W. BANKS

═══◈═══

BAT MASTERSON WAS A BLUE-EYED DANDY WHO FAVORED starched shirts, derbies, Colt pistols with carved pearl grips, and saloons where bawdy women pranced around gaming tables piled with money.

With these character traits and his close friendship with Wyatt Earp, Masterson inevitably showed up in Tombstone.

He arrived there on February 8, 1881, just nine months before the fight near the O.K. Corral.

Although Masterson's role in the epic Earp-Clanton feud was by no means pivotal, it was greater than is commonly supposed.

And for those who like to wonder what might have been, his short stay in Tombstone poses some tantalizing questions.

Bartholomew Masterson — a name he later changed to William Barclay — was born to farming parents in Quebec, Canada, on November 26, 1853. From there the family moved to Illinois, Missouri, and, in 1870, to Sedgwick County, Kansas.

Like Wyatt Earp, the young Masterson sought adventure. He found it, working on the Atchison, Topeka and Santa Fe Railroad, hunting buffalo, and working as a civilian scout under Col. Nelson A. Miles.

BAT MASTERSON, CIRCA 1885.

Masterson went to Dodge City in 1875. There he renewed his friendship with another ex-buffalo hunter — a skinny, tough, no-nonsense fellow from Monmouth, Illinois, named Wyatt Earp.

The two eventually served side by side as Dodge City lawmen during one of the frontier's wildest times, forming a bond of mutual admiration that lasted a lifetime.

But their personalities couldn't have been more different. While Earp was tight-lipped and aggressive, Masterson was good-natured, talkative, and popular, a well-dressed rogue in a cattle camp known for dust, mud, and blood.

Even so, no one mistook his flamboyance for weakness. As the *Dodge City Times* wrote during Masterson's successful campaign for sheriff in November, 1877:

"He knew how to gather in the sinners, is qualified to fill the office, and, if elected, will never shrink from danger."

Earp respected Masterson's guts as well as his skill with a six-gun. After Earp moved to Tombstone, he asked Masterson to join him. Masterson was to deal faro and keep order at the Oriental Saloon, where the gaming tables Wyatt owned were being harassed by ruffians hired by business rivals.

Accompanied by Luke Short, described as a sawed-off gambler and whiskey peddler, Masterson responded to his friend's call and made the arduous journey west by train and stagecoach.

It was on this trip that Bat met and befriended William H. Stilwell, who was traveling to Arizona to begin his duties as associate judge for the Territory.

Neither man could have imagined the future. Little more than a year later, Earp would be leading a federal posse in pursuit of the murderers of his brother, Morgan — and carrying in his pocket warrants signed by Stilwell.

If not for Masterson, the new judge might not have reached Arizona Territory at all. Stilwell's demeanor and dress made him a ready target for the hard-bitten men they encountered along the way.

In his description of the trip, fellow passenger George T. Buffum wrote that Stilwell "wore a silk hat, the first to be tolerated in New Mexico without a few shots being taken at it," and his "only weapon was a silk umbrella."

At Deming, New Mexico, Masterson intervened when Stilwell was harassed by a group of irate railroad workers. The railroad workers had been forced to wait while the judge finished eating.

One of the workers pointed at Stilwell and said: "See that long, lank cuss fresh from New York just filling himself as though he had been through a famine, while we railroad boys have to wait?"

Buffum said that Masterson, carrying a Sharps' rifle and two revolvers, glowered at the men before cutting "loose with a burst of colorful, Dodge City, whorehouse invective."

Buffum wrote: "Masterson, in great wrath and with

resounding oaths, resented this insult to his friend, and ended with, 'Buffum, you just take the first vacant seat and let these sons of the burro wait.'"

On the last leg of his trip, the rough stagecoach ride from Benson to Tombstone, Masterson also met Wells Fargo messenger Bob Paul.

Richard DeArment, in his book *Bat Masterson, The Man, The Legend*, said Paul used the occasion to tell Masterson the story of the Earps' first year in the Territory, the threatened outbreak of a gamblers' war, and the more ominous rise of a cowboy gang of rustlers and killers.

Less than three weeks after his arrival, Masterson learned the dangers of Tombstone firsthand. In the Oriental on the morning of February 25, the well-known gambler and drinking man Charlie Storms traded hot words with Luke Short.

In his series on gunfighters published in the April 1907 edition of *Human Life Magazine*, Masterson wrote that "both men were about to pull their pistols when I jumped between them and grabbed Storms, at the same time requesting Luke not to shoot."

Masterson, an old friend of Storms, walked the drunken gambler back to his room. Thinking the incident was over, Bat returned to the Oriental and met Short on the sidewalk at the corner of Fifth and Allen streets.

"I was just explaining to Luke that Storms was a very decent sort of man," Masterson wrote, "when, lo and behold! There he stood before us. Without saying a word, he took hold of Luke's arm and pulled him off the sidewalk, where he had been standing, at the same time pulling his pistol, a Colt's cut-off, 45 caliber, single action; but . . . he was too slow, although he succeeded in getting his pistol out. Luke stuck the muzzle of his own pistol against Storms' heart and pulled the trigger.

"The bullet tore the heart asunder, and as he was falling, Luke shot him again. Storms was dead when he hit the ground."

William Cox, Luke Short's biographer, wrote that Storms'

killing was the first shot in the war between the Earps and the cowboys.

That's a questionable assertion. More likely, it was part of the gamblers' war that Earp feared when he summoned Masterson to town.

But there was no doubt that the March 15, 1881, holdup of a stagecoach between Tombstone and Benson, in which driver Bud Philpot and passenger Peter Roerig were killed, was the work of four members of the cowboy gang.

Masterson, able to read sign like an Indian, was deputized by Earp to join a posse that included Virgil and Morgan Earp, Bob Paul, a second Wells Fargo agent, Cochise County Sheriff Johnny Behan, and his deputy, Billy Breakenridge.

It was a frustrating 10-day hunt over more than 300 miles resulting in only one arrest. DeArment wrote that the hardships of the ride reminded Masterson of his days as a scout with Colonel Miles in 1874:

"Both men and horses suffered from fatigue and thirst, but their horses gave out first. Bat's animal fell dead under him. He was forced to give up the chase."

The Earp party's frustration turned to fury when they returned and learned that Luther King, captured by the Earps and Masterson on March 19 and taken back to Tombstone by Behan, had escaped custody.

Suspicions were strong that Behan, an enemy of Wyatt Earp and friend of the cowboy gang, had allowed King to get away. This unholy alliance of Behan's would continue in the coming year, forcing Wyatt Earp to settle the feud his own way, outside the law.

But Masterson wasn't around for that trouble, even though some of the wildly erroneous news reports after the O.K. Corral fight named him as a participant. Although off by six months, that fiction proved surprisingly resilient.

After about 60 days in Tombstone, Masterson received two urgent telegrams informing him that his brother, Jim, a Kansas saloon keeper, was in a dangerous fix and needed help.

He left Tombstone immediately, arriving in Dodge City on April 16, 1881.

But Masterson's role in the Wyatt Earp story was not over yet. The two men met again, in Trinidad, Colorado, in May, 1882.

In the previous weeks, Wyatt and his brother, Warren, Doc Holliday, and four other men had coldly gunned down several members of the cowboy gang.

Now Earp and Holliday were fugitives wanted for murder. The matter was further complicated by Holliday's arrest in Denver on May 15, 1882. Colorado authorities were holding him for extradition to Arizona, which surely would have resulted in his assassination.

Earp asked Masterson to get Holliday out of jail. Masterson, then the marshal at Trinidad, used his pull to produce a phony warrant for Doc's arrest on a bunco charge out of Pueblo, Colorado.

When Masterson and Pueblo's marshal went to the Denver jail to spring Holliday, the sheriff there correctly figured the warrant was nothing but a scheme to spirit Holliday away. He refused to give up his man.

But Masterson wouldn't quit. With the Denver papers printing sensational tales of Holliday's past, Masterson stood up and defended the man: "I tell you that all this talk is wrong about Holliday. I know him well. He is a dentist and a good one. . . . an enemy of the lawless element."

He also attacked the man who arrested Holliday as a fraud, which turned out to be true. Perry Mallan had presented himself to Denver authorities as an Arizona lawman, but he was actually a petty swindler posing as a cop.

It was a bizarre episode in which everyone, including Masterson, was lying. The truth was that Masterson, like most other people, thoroughly disliked Holliday, calling him perverse, mean, and "a weakling who could not have whipped a healthy 15-year-old boy."

Masterson was a generally honest lawman. But because

of his loyalty and friendship with Wyatt Earp, he was willing to lie and subvert the law to save the life of a man he despised.

Masterson wrangled a private meeting with Colorado Gov. Frederick Pitkin that resulted in a denial of the extradition request, due mainly to the Pueblo warrant.

As for the bunco charge, Bat wrote in the May 1907 issue of *Human Life* that Holliday "always managed to have his case put off . . . and, by furnishing a new bond, in every instance would be released again."

Holliday was still under bond for the phony indictment when he died five years later.

Had Masterson stayed in Tombstone, that same loyalty almost certainly would have drawn him deeper into the Earp-Clanton feud. It might even have placed him at the O.K. Corral on that fateful October afternoon.

It's interesting to speculate how events might have played out then. Could the addition of his guns to the Earp party brought more cowboys to town, increasing the bloodshed? Or perhaps his easy nature would have tempered Earp's belligerence and staved off the hostilities altogether.

As it was, Masterson went on to live the life of a vagabond gambler and freelance lawman. In 1891, his notoriously roving eye settled on Emma Walters, a blond dancing girl who he married and stayed with for the rest of his life.

Masterson's last job was at the *New York Morning Telegraph*, where he was a smart and tough sportswriter specializing in prizefighting. He died at his desk on October 25, 1921, at age 67, one day before the 40th anniversary of the gunfight he missed.

CHAPTER SEVENTEEN

HUNTING THE BUNTLINE SPECIAL

Why vehemently debate whether five particular Colt .45s ever existed? When one of those guns was supposed to be Wyatt Earp's custom revolver during his Tombstone days, romantics and skeptics alike have plenty to say.

BY LEO W. BANKS

ONE OF THE MOST PERSISTENT LEGENDS SURROUNDING Wyatt Earp is that of the Buntline Special, the extra-long-barreled Colt .45 revolver that dime novelist Ned Buntline supposedly presented to Earp as a gift. Stuart Lake, Wyatt's biographer, called the gun the "excalibur" of weapons, and he wasn't far off. Like Arthur's legendary sword, this one revolver has gained almost mythic status as the weapon that the great marshal used to tame the streets and saloons of Tombstone.

Even so, many Western historians have dismissed the Special as a tall tale more worthy of laughter than serious consideration. But new evidence indicates that such a judgment might be wrong. Earp historian Lee A. Silva, author of *Wyatt Earp: A Biography of the Legend*, has spent years compiling a trail of clues that he believes points in only one direction. And while he cannot hold aloft the ultimate proof, an actual Buntline Special, Silva is convinced the mystery has been solved.

"When I started this, I had doubts," said the Long Beach, California, writer and firearms expert. "But now I'm absolutely, 100 percent certain the story is true. Buntline really did present such a gun to Earp."

Buntline was the author of more than 400 dime novels and one of the 19th century's most famous men. He was a rogue, rascal, and liar. But in analyzing the truth of this legend, it is Stuart Lake's character at issue, not Buntline's. Those who doubt the Special's existence contend that Lake simply invented the gun to sell his 1931 book, *Wyatt Earp, Frontier Marshal.*

That biography's 1930 serialization in the *Saturday Evening Post* constitutes the first published mention of the Buntline Special. Lake wrote that Buntline heard of Earp's prowess as a lawman and sought him out in Dodge City in 1876. After plying Earp and four other peace officers — Bat Masterson, Bill Tilghman, Charlie Bassett, and Neil Brown — for their frontier stories, Buntline was so grateful that he arranged to give the men gifts.

"He sent to the Colt factory," Lake wrote, "for five special forty-five caliber six-guns of regulation single-action style, but with barrels four inches longer than standard — a foot in length — making them eighteen inches overall. Each gun had a demountable walnut rifle stock, with a thumbscrew arrangement to fit the weapon for a shoulder-piece in long-range shooting."

The story received a boost 24 years later with the television series, *The Life and Legend of Wyatt Earp.* From 1955 to 1961, actor Hugh O'Brian, as Wyatt Earp, carried a Buntline. The show's popularity flooded the market with plastic Specials, and the Colt company produced and sold thousands of real-life, long-barreled Colts.

But nonbelievers say the craze, like the gun, was created out of thin air. William Shillingberg, in his 1976 book on the subject, called the Buntline tale "a bizarre melange of truth and fiction, documentation and speculation, misrepresentation of facts through ignorance and through deliberate distortion."

The case against the legend has rested, mainly, on two questions: If the story is true, why are there no production or shipping records from the Colt factory? And why would Buntline give the guns to these five men, when two of them, at the time of the alleged presentation, weren't even lawmen yet?

Another question: Why give to lawmen an awkward, long-barreled gun when a standard model could be much more easily drawn and handled?

In response, Silva argues that Lake would never have spent so much precious research time hunting for Earp's Buntline if the story was his own invention. Lake believed the old marshal gave his gun to Charlie Hoxie, the man with whom Earp operated the Dexter Saloon in Nome, Alaska, in 1900 and 1901. Lake wrote numerous letters to old-timers and editors in Alaska searching for it. He tried desperately to find Masterson's Buntline Special, too.

Would a man perpetrating a hoax go to such lengths? Would he agonize, as Lake did in research letters and notes, over whether the barrel was 10 or 12 inches long?

As for the absence of company records, Silva has an explanation: The Colt company didn't keep production records on guns leaving the factory until 1909. And the company's shipping records are notoriously sketchy.

"We have no doubt but that a record was made of the special revolvers furnished Ned Buntline in 1876," Colt company historian Arthur L. Ulrich wrote to Lake in a 1929 letter.

Having said that — seeming to acknowledge the guns' existence — Ulrich went on to say he just couldn't find the records.

Silva says the second question posed a false assumption. "He [Buntline] didn't give them Buntlines because they were lawmen who told great stories," he says. "It finally dawned on me, he did it because they were professional buffalo hunters."

His explanation dates to 1872 and 1873, when William F. "Buffalo Bill" Cody became a celebrity from the success of a Buntline play called *The Scouts of the Prairie*. The play made buckets of money on its multicity tour, but then Cody ended his involvement with the troupe.

Buntline was without the steady money to which he'd

become accustomed. Eager to produce another moneymaking play as sensational as *Scouts*, he presented the long-barreled Specials to the five men, hoping to turn one or more into the next Buffalo Bill.

Buntline had taken the same tack when wooing Cody. From an old newspaper article, unearthed by Buntline expert Robert Pepper, Silva learned that Buntline convinced Cody to go on stage by giving him a custom-made deer rifle.

"Buntline loved exotic weapons, had contacts at the Colt factory, and he'd made a similar presentation to Cody," Silva said. "It all fits. A long-range target pistol is an appropriate gift to give a buffalo hunter. But it wouldn't be to a lawman."

Here, the pro-Buntline case takes a turn involving Buckskin Frank Leslie, a notorious figure in Tombstone in the early 1880s. A Connecticut library's files hold a letter from Buckskin Frank to Colt, ordering a frontier model revolver with a 12-inch barrel, "browned, superior finished throughout with carved ivory handle."

Silva raises two intriguing facts about that request. At the time, Buckskin Frank and Wyatt Earp worked together at Tombstone's Oriental Saloon. And the letter's date, January 14, 1881, is the same day Earp held off a mob bent on lynching gambler Johnny-Behind-The-Deuce.

Even Earp author Bob Boze Bell, a Buntline skeptic, said the coincidence raised by the letter is too great to ignore.

"It doesn't explain why there was no publicity about the presentation at the time it was made, which is my biggest problem," Bell said. "But Leslie's letter sure puts the legend within the realm of possibility."

Leslie wasn't the only Tombstone resident to order a long-barreled Colt. Silva found factory records showing that Colt also shipped a long-barreled revolver to S.L. Hart, a Tombstone gunsmith. The gun was sent May 12, 1882, six weeks after Earp left Tombstone for the final time.

Writing in the journal of the National Association for Outlaw and Lawman History, Silva argued: "When it is assumed that there were a total of less than 50 extra-long-barreled Colts ordered from the Colt factory from 1873 until 1941, what are the odds of two men in a town like Tombstone, with a population of about 6,000, deciding they also wanted extra-long-barreled Colts unless they had seen Wyatt packing one?"

Silva was aided in much of his research by Jeff Morey, another noted Earp historian. While he agrees the legend is most likely true, he differs from Silva on two key points.

Morey doubts that Ned Buntline was even in Dodge in 1876. However, the author was in Philadelphia that fall for the Centennial Exposition, where Colt first displayed its revolver-carbine and, presumably, where Buntline first saw the long-barreled Specials.

But that fall visit was after the supposed gungiving, which, according to Lake, occurred in the summer.

Morey says Buntline's presentation probably occurred in 1878. That year, an entertainer named Dora Hand was murdered in Dodge, and the posse that pursued her included four of the five men who were given Buntlines.

In his research notes for *Frontier Marshal*, Lake revealed that he initially wrote, based on Wyatt's failing memory, that the Hand murder occurred in 1876. He caught that error before going to print. However, Morey believes Lake failed then to change the date of the presentation as well. As for the fifth posse man, Morey theorizes that Wyatt's recollection again failed and that he substituted Neil Brown for William Duffey.

Of course, Buntline proponents have yet to actually recover even one of the presentation guns. The weapons given to Neil Brown and Charlie Bassett seem to have disappeared. Bill Tilghman's gun was reportedly stolen, while Masterson found his Buntline unwieldy, had the barrel cut down, and gave it to a friend. Earp's gun vanished along with Charlie Hoxie.

Finally, at the O.K. Corral was Earp packing his long-barreled Colt that day? Lake said yes, and the inquest testimony of a butcher named A. Bauer, who witnessed the fight, seemed to confirm it. Asked to describe the weapon Earp was carrying two hours before the fight when he buffaloed Tom McLaury, Bauer said: "It seemed to me an old pistol, pretty large, 14 or 16 inches long."

From an eyewitness, especially a butcher, who'd know the length of a knife, and probably a gun as well, that's strong stuff. But doubters wonder why Earp, intent on arresting desperate men, would carry such an unwieldy gun. From Earp's own testimony, we know he wasn't holstered that day and kept his firearm in the pocket of his coat. A long weapon couldn't fit in a standard pocket, a fact that should, by itself, dismiss the possibility he had a Buntline.

But another twist: Several historians have written that the coat Earp wore that afternoon had a specially made, leather-lined inside pocket, suitable for holding such a weapon. Especially true if it had a 10-inch barrel, which, experts say, isn't the least unwieldy. Silva and Morey agree that the weapon probably was a 10-incher. Of the 30 extra-long-barreled guns Colt is known to have produced between 1876 and 1890, only one had a 12-inch barrel. The remainder measured either 16 or 10 inches.

So the legend deepens, and the theories are debated. After all, Arizona is a place of legends, and no one has created more than Wyatt Earp.

PHOTOGRAPH CREDITS:

CHAPTER ONE
PAGE 9   School children. Arizona Historical Society/Tucson, AHS#5210.
PAGE 11   Eddie Foy. Arizona Historical Society/Tucson, AHS#44684.
PAGE 13   Baseball teams. Arizona Department of Library, Archives and Public Records, Archives Division, Phoenix, #97-0216.
PAGE 14   Prospector. Arizona Historical Society/Tucson, AHS#541.
PAGE 17   John Slaughter. Arizona Department of Library, Archives and Public Records, Archives Division, Phoenix, #97-7876.

CHAPTER TWO
PAGE 20   Ed Schieffelin. Arizona Department of Library, Archives and Public Records, Archives Division, Phoenix, #97-8446.
PAGE 23   Richard Gird. Arizona Department of Library, Archives and Public Records, Archives Division, Phoenix, #97-6368.
PAGE 26   Alaska Prospecting Party. Arizona Department of Library, Archives and Public Records, Archives Division, Phoenix, #97-2640.

CHAPTER THREE
PAGE 31   John P. Clum. Arizona Department of Library, Archives and Public Records, Archives Division, Phoenix, #97-7477.

CHAPTER FOUR
PAGE 38   George Parsons. Arizona Historical Society/Tucson, AHS#1934.

CHAPTER FIVE
PAGE 45   Wyatt Earp. Department of Southwest Studies, Maricopa Community Colleges.
PAGE 46   Morgan Earp. Department of Southwest Studies, Maricopa Community Colleges.
PAGE 49   Virgil Earp. Department of Southwest Studies, Maricopa Community Colleges.
PAGE 50   Feud victims. The Arizona Historical Society/Tucson, AHS#17483.

CHAPTER SIX
PAGE 54   Big Nose Kate. Arizona Historical Society/Tucson, AHS#44682.
PAGE 57   John "Doc" Holliday. Arizona Historical Society/Tucson, AHS#54797.

CHAPTER SEVEN
PAGE 63   John Behan. Arizona Department of Library, Archives and Public Records, Archives Division, Phoenix, #97-6520.

CHAPTER EIGHT
PAGE 69   C.S. Fly. Arizona Department of Library, Archives and Public Records, Archives Division, Phoenix, #96-3879.
PAGE 70   Mollie Fly. Arizona Department of Library, Archives and Public Records, Archives Division, Phoenix, #94-0011.
PAGE 73   Apaches in Mexico. Arizona Department of Library, Archives and Public Records, Archives Division, Phoenix, #97-2621.

CHAPTER NINE
PAGE 78   Ike Clanton. Arizona Historical Society/Tucson, AHS#24366.
PAGE 81   Newman Clanton. Arizona Historical Society/Tucson, AHS#40882.

C.S. FLY PHOTOGRAPHED THIS VIEW OF TOMBSTONE, LOOKING TO THE NORTH, CIRCA 1885. NOTE THE FIRE DAMAGE TO FLY'S GLASS PLATE NEGATIVE.

STALWART WOMEN
Frontier Stories of Indomitable Spirit

Tough enough to walk barefoot through 15 miles of desert and cactus forest. Strong enough to fell a man with one jaw-crunching blow. Intuitive enough to break camp minutes before 40-foot-high floodwaters crashed in. Wily enough to con the U.S. Army.

You say you know all the tales of the frontier's mountain men and buffalo hunters, lawmen and gunmen, rustlers, cowboys, warriors, and generals? You haven't known the full excitement of the Old West until you read the adventures of the unique women who left cities and towns behind to plunge into the harsh unknown.

Life was a struggle, demanding pluck and endurance to extremes sometimes difficult to imagine. Yet the gritty accounts told here are not fiction, but the gripping factual descriptions of tough, steel-spined women. They forged homes and businesses in the hostile wilderness, fought Indians and taught schools, charmed their way through war zones, and commandeered arduous rescue missions. These survivors didn't buckle when disaster struck, and disaster struck often.

Sixth in the Wild West Collection, *Stalwart Women* is a fast-paced read, 15 harrowing stories by Tucson author Leo W. Banks. Start in the middle or read them all straight through, you'll find that each chapter stands on its own as a riveting portrait of sheer adventure.

Softcover. 144 pages. Illustrated with historical photographs.

#AWWP8 $7.95

Coming in March 1999

Ordering Information on Page 144

DAYS OF DESTINY
Fate Beckons Desperados & Lawmen

Many a newcomer journeyed West intent on molding his own future, grabbing life with both hands and producing opportunity. Shifty or bold, desperate or noble, given a trusty horse, a gun, and occasional friends, any man might stand a chance. But every chain of events has one single day, perhaps a fleeting moment, when fate first points a decisive finger and the course of history changes. Delve into this collection of 20 Wild West tales of how real-life desperados and lawmen faced momentous days that changed their lives forever. Does the outlaw finally dance to his doom? Will the lynch mob hang the little weasel that just killed a man? Does the kidnapped boy stay with the Apaches who stole him? Will the young mother become a stagecoach robber? Look back through time to see if you can spot when destiny dealt the final hand.

Softcover. 144 pages. #ADAP6 $7.95

MANHUNTS & MASSACRES

Cleverly staged ambushes, horrific massacres, and dogged pursuits catapult the reader into days of savagery on the Arizona frontier. If life was hard, death came even harder: A bungled robbery leads to murder. Arizona's largest manhunt imprisons two brothers unjustly. Sleeping cowboys are ambushed in Guadalupe Canyon. Bloodstained cash traps a family's desperate killer. Reading through these 18 accounts, you'll join the posses in hot pursuit across the roughest terrain and outwit the most suspicious of fugitive outlaws. From the vicious to the valiant, each true story will convince you — the good old days were a challenge that few of us could survive!

Softcover. 144 pages. #AMMP7 $7.95

Ordering Information on Page 144

THEY LEFT THEIR MARK:
Heroes and Rogues of Arizona History

Indians, scouts, ranchers, and mountain men are vividly remembered here in 16 true stories of Western adventure. Before Arizona Territory was ever mapped or named, its rugged terrain and extreme temperatures demanded much of the explorers who reached it. Generations passed, yet even as more and more people came to the Southwest, the land remained rugged, harsh. Those whose names are remembered were individualists who left their unique stamp — good or bad — on Arizona's history: Alchesay, the Apache who successfuly led his people in war and in peace; Dr. Goodfellow, the Tombstone surgeon who became a national expert on bullet wounds; swindler James Addison Reavis, who almost made himself a Spanish baron with an Arizona kingdom; and many more.

Softcover. 144 pages. Black and white historical photographs. **#ATMP7 $7.95**

THE LAW OF THE GUN
by Marshall Trimble

Recounting the colorful lives and careers of gunfighters, lawmen, and outlaws, historian and author Marshall Trimble examines the mystique of the Old West and the role that guns have played with that fascination. Tools of survival as well as deadly weapons, guns on the American frontier came to symbolize the guts and independence that people idealized in their Western heroes — even when those "heroes" were cold-blooded killers. With the deft touch of a master storyteller, Trimble recounts the macabre humor of digging up one dead gunslinger to deliver his last shot of whiskey, the intensity of the Arizona Rangers who faced death down a gun barrel every time they pursued a crook, and the vengeful aftermath of Wyatt Earp's showdown in Tombstone. Each gripping tale will make you want to read more of how guns determined life in the West.

Softcover. 192 pages. Black and white historical photographs. **#AGNP7 $8.95**

Cow Pie Ain't No Dish You Take to the County Fair

That's just one of the cowboy-style witticisms and homespun truths that will get you giggling over a helping of Western-flavored humor. Accented by Arizona artist Jim Willoughby's whimsical cartoons, this hand-sized collection of 165 jokes, riddles, one-liners, and cowpuncher proverbs will make you laugh until you're punchy. The whole family can enjoy a light, friendly look at what life just might really be like out on the range.

Softcover. 144 pages. **#ACWP7 $6.95**

Ordering Information
To order these and other books and products write to:
Arizona Highways, 2039 West Lewis Avenue, Phoenix, AZ 85009-2893.
Or send a fax to 602-254-4505.
Or call toll-free nationwide 1-800-543-5432.
(In the Phoenix area or outside the U.S., call 602-258-1000.)
Visit us at http://www.arizhwys.com to order online.